THE ULTIMATE GUIDE TO
MIXED MARTIAL ARTS

THE ULTIMATE GUIDE TO
MIXED MARTIAL ARTS

Compiled by Jon Sattler

Edited by Raymond Horwitz,
Jeannine Santiago, Jon Sattler and Jon Thibault

Graphic Design by John Bodine

Front Cover Photos:
Chuck Liddell, Randy Couture and Bas Rutten by Rick Hustead
B.J. Penn by Sara Fogan
Matt Hughes by Fernando Escovar
Rickson Gracie and Tito Ortiz from the *Black Belt* Archives

Back Cover Photo:
Dan Henderson by Greg Wetzel

©2007 Black Belt Communications LLC
All Rights Reserved
Printed in the United States of America
Library of Congress Control Number: 2007928718
ISBN-10: 0-89750-159-4
ISBN-13: 978-0-89750-159-0

First Printing 2007

BLACK BELT BOOKS
A Division of **OHARA ▯ PUBLICATIONS, INC.**
World Leader in Martial Arts Publications

FOREWORD

You can't teach someone to want to fight. He has to like fighting.

—Chuck "The Iceman" Liddell

If you're reading this book, chances are you like fighting. Perhaps you live for the intoxicating rush of combat and revel in modern-day gladiator games. Or you derive countless hours of pleasure from contemplating the more esoteric aspects of the sport: the beauty of a well-executed armbar from the guard, the serene, glazed-over expression of a fighter slipping into unconsciousness as his neck and carotid arteries are squeezed like a wet ham.

Or maybe you just like punching people in the face. Which, one supposes, has its own innate beauty.

The mixed martial arts aren't for everyone. The sight of trained combatants striving for supremacy in a bloodstained octagon often causes lesser men to look away in shame and self-loathing. But you're different. You understand both the elegance and horror of the cage.

You're the reason we made *The Ultimate Guide to Mixed Martial Arts*.

—*Jon Sattler*

CONTENTS

WHO IS RICKSON GRACIE, AND WHY DO PEOPLE THINK HE'S THE BEST FIGHTER IN THE WORLD?
An Interview With Royce Gracie's Big Brother

Interview by Dr. Stephen V. Hoyt and Jim Coleman • September 1995

Martial artists have heard plenty in recent months about Brazilian-*jujutsu* stylist Royce Gracie, who has won three Ultimate Fighting Championship titles and was named *Black Belt's* 1994 Competitor of the Year. But the name Rickson Gracie is also popping up with increasing regularity—and for good reason.

Rickson Gracie, Royce's older brother, is considered by many martial arts pundits to be the best fighter in the Gracie family, if not the world. The stocky 34-year-old has collected $110,000 in prize money by winning the first two Vale Tudo Fighting Championship tournaments in Tokyo, and he has been approached by promoters of American no-holds-barred events. But, for reasons he explains in this interview, the 5-foot-9-inch, 185-pounder has yet to compete in the United States.

Black Belt: Last April, you won your second consecutive Vale Tudo Fighting Championship title, which is a virtually no-holds-barred event in Tokyo, similar to the UFC in the United States. What does *vale tudo* mean?

Rickson Gracie: "Vale tudo" is a Portuguese and Brazilian word meaning "everything goes." The tournament brings back the spirit of doing everything you want.

BB: What are the rule differences between the UFC and the Vale Tudo event?

Gracie: The UFC fights have time limits. In the Vale Tudo, there are eight-minute rounds. You go for eight minutes, then you go another eight minutes until one fighter taps or passes out. And we wear gloves, more to protect the fighter who wears the glove than the guy who receives the punch, because you can get infected or break your hand. The glove is not that thick; it weighs maybe 8 ounces. And with this glove, you can hold, grab or punch.

BB: Are you allowed to bite at the Vale Tudo?

Gracie: No.

BB: Can you gouge the opponent's eyes?

Gracie: No.

BB: Head-butt?

Gracie: You can use head butts on the floor. You can basically do whatever you want. You can choke, punch, elbow, or use your knees.

BB: How did you defeat Japanese wrestler Yoshihisa Yamamoto, the first of your three opponents at the Vale Tudo tournament?

Gracie: The match went for about 20 minutes because he held the ropes for the first two rounds. Then, in the third round, I moved back, I waited for him to exchange punches with me, then I took him to the floor and finished the fight.

Many people consider Brazilian-jujutsu stylist Rickson Gracie to be not only the best fighter in the Gracie family but in the entire world.

BB: How did you finish him?

Gracie: I choked him out. I choked out all three of my opponents.

BB: Who was your second fight against?

Gracie: Koichiro Kimura. That match lasted about three or four minutes.

BB: Who did you defeat in the championship bout?

Gracie: A Japanese shootwrestler named Yuki Nakai. He's a light guy, about 165 pounds. It was over in about four minutes.

BB: How did the predominantly Japanese fans feel about you beating three of their fighters?

Gracie: I felt the whole crowd was against me from the moment I fought Yamamoto. He's a famous pro wrestler over there. The crowd was all for him.

BB: Are you pretty popular in Japan—except when you're fighting a Japanese opponent?

Gracie: I think so. The Japanese give me very special recognition. They really respect tradition, and they love jujutsu. I'm becoming a new sensation over there.

BB: Why haven't you competed at the UFC? The championship purse is about the same as the Vale Tudo tournament.

Gracie: I don't see why I should get involved in the UFC if Royce is already taking care of business. The idea was to put Royce in the UFC to give him some exposure. And I think it's been very good for him. I'm happy for him.

BB: Would you consider competing in NHB events in the United States if the price was right?

Gracie: I'm open for any event. It all depends on the business aspect, the prize, and the level of the participants.

BB: Do you think the skill level of the competitors at the UFC has been high?

Gracie: I think the level is OK. They're good fighters.

BB: Many people think you are the best fighter in the Gracie family. Do you agree?

Gracie: I don't consider myself to be the best. Other people consider me.

BB: Some people have gone so far as to suggest you are the best fighter in the world. Have you heard those claims?

Gracie: Yes.

BB: What do you think when you hear that?

Gracie: [That I better] keep training hard. To keep this kind of reputation is a very heavy load on my back. I'll try my best to stay with it.

BB: What is the difference between traditional jujutsu and your brand of Brazilian jujutsu?

Gracie: Traditional jujutsu focuses on hip throws and wrist locks. We focus on real fighting situations, looking at punching, kicking, head butts, elbows, throws and finishing holds, both with a judo *gi* and without a judo gi. We focus pretty much on no-rules situations, with a lot of realism.

BB: If you always trained completely realistically, you wouldn't have many students left. Where do you draw the line between realism and training?

Gracie: The realism is in the way you approach the maneuvers, not in the violence with which you execute the techniques. You can train very realistically, trying everything you want, but you don't have to be mean and try to hurt somebody. We can train at a slow pace and still do everything we want to do. Our training is different than a boxer, who just exchanges punches, either fast or slow. But we cover all the different aspects of real fighting; there's no limitations. And any time we get close to a dangerous situation, we let the opponent tap out.

BB: How many hours per day do you train?

Gracie: I teach and train from eight to 10 hours a day. I have my own personal fitness program that I made up. It combines breathing, flexibility, strength, speed, cardiovascular endurance, muscle toning, balance and coordination.

BB: What do you focus on at your jujutsu seminars?

Gracie: I try to teach a balance of training hard and being gentle. I also hope to teach seminar students to love each other. Because everything we try to do must have some love in it. I believe the martial arts should have feelings. Toughness is not the way you act, but how you do something. I always try to be as nice as I can be, and I try to teach this same approach to the students.

BB: Why do you sometimes refer to your style as "Gracie" instead of jujutsu?

Gracie: In Brazil, there is no such thing as Gracie jujutsu. The only source of jujutsu there is from my family. My family learned jujutsu from a Japanese guy in Brazil and developed it from there. But once we moved to the United States about 15 years ago, we started calling it Gracie jujutsu, just to distinguish it from other styles of jujutsu.

BB: Do you incorporate any of the Japanese jujutsu philosophy or techniques into your system?

Gracie: No. I never learned anything of value in jujutsu from the Japanese. Nothing. In Brazil, people don't care about the tradition in a martial art; they just want to learn to fight. People there have a different attitude. Once you come with some kind of martial art, you have to be able to prove how it works. You get challenges where people call you names and want to fight you. People there don't want to learn some style in a civilized sense.

BB: What is your opinion of Olympic-style wrestling, and is it a viable form of self-defense?

Gracie: Wrestling is a style where you develop an excellent sense of balance, and where you have some options to throw your opponent and keep the top position, because that's the main part of the game—to control and pin your opponent. These types of wrestlers are very tough within the rules they practice, but they don't do any training on how to block kicks, how to use submission holds, and things like that.

BB: Have you ever trained with any good wrestlers?

Gracie: Yes. I had the opportunity to train with 1988 Olympic gold-medalist Mark Shultz at the University of Utah. I wrestled with him, and there was no doubt that when we wrestled, he could maintain the top position. But whenever he made a mistake, I made him tap out. And he couldn't make me tap out.

BB: How many people are authorized to teach Gracie-style jujutsu?

Gracie: I don't know anybody besides my family who is capable of teaching Gracie jujutsu. But I'm working on spreading our system by teaching certain instructors. But this takes time, and I'm very concerned about making sure they maintain top quality.

BB: Does your style have a belt-ranking system?

Gracie: Yes. The system starts with white, then progresses to blue, purple, brown, and finally black belt. All of these steps take an average of 10 years. If someone is very good, he can make it in seven years.

BB: Are any of your students as talented as you and your brothers?

Gracie: No, because we have a lifetime of experience and they don't.

BB: There are four Gracie brothers—yourself, Royce, Rorion and Relson—in the United States. How many more members are there in the Gracie family?

Gracie: All together, the Gracie family has at least 500 people.

BB: So the Gracie name will not die out soon?

Gracie: Oh, that's for sure.

BB: Does your father, Helio, still set policy and intervene in the family's martial arts business?

Gracie: He intervenes in a gentle way, yes. My dad always tries to give us advice. But at a point, we are grown up enough so we know what's best. He just gives his love and respect and knowledge in his advice to us. But we are our own masters now.

BB: It seems that all of the Gracies place tremendous value on the family unit.

Gracie: Yes, absolutely. Everything I have is due to my family. You cannot achieve any kind of balance without being part of a family. A family, I think, gives you an approach to life in which problems can be dealt with easier. You don't have the same type of commitment when you are single. When you're not married, you want to party and do things that probably aren't as smart.

BB: Do you try to get that message across to your American students?

Gracie: Yes, absolutely. In Brazil, people devote more time to their family than the people in America do. I think family is essential for reaching your goals. The highest inspiration I have comes from my family.

BB: What do you think about when you enter the ring to fight?

Gracie: I try to release myself from any responsibilities or burdens when I fight. I surrender to God. I don't think about what's going to happen if I don't win. I do my best and don't worry about the results. I don't let the pressures get to me.

BB: Did you ever consider a career in anything other than fighting?

Gracie: I thought maybe I'd become a teacher, but it didn't make any sense to continue my schooling because I was making good money already from jujutsu. So I quit school and became a full-time jujutsu instructor.

BB: Do you worry about your opponents when you fight, or do you just focus on your own performance?

Gracie: You have to concentrate on what you're doing and not get distracted by one type of fighter or another. You just do your best and put everything in God's hands.

BB: How much longer do you plan to compete at tournaments?

Gracie: I'm in my prime. I do well at what I'm doing and feel wasted if I don't compete. I am always looking for opportunities to show my skills. You must have strength, agility, endurance and flexibility. Once I feel that I don't have all those things, then I'll stop. I am going to try to compete forever.

HOW TO APPLY AND ESCAPE FROM THE GUILLOTINE CHOKE
Don't Lose Your Head When Your Neck Is on the Line

by Bart Smith • Photos courtesy of Bart Smith • August 1996

If you have watched any of the no-holds-barred tournaments on television the past few years, you have likely witnessed the use of a powerful choking technique called the "guillotine." This technique is not only very effective, but it is also easy to apply in a variety of fighting situations.

The guillotine is most often used against an opponent who shoots in for a takedown or ducks his head to avoid a punch. A properly executed guillotine at this moment will place the opponent in a front head lock. Use the bony part of your forearm to choke your adversary and hyperextend the vertebrae in his neck.

To apply the guillotine choke when standing, you must get a snug hold around the opponent's neck and then arch your back, pulling his head away from the body, beyond its normal range of motion. Once again, the "blade" of your forearm inflicts painful pressure to the opponent's throat and neck, likely causing unconsciousness, spinal injury, or both.

The guillotine is not the most highly technical choke available, but if applied against an unwitting adversary, it can be as devastating as any choking technique in the martial arts. Just ask Ray Wizard, Johnny Rhodes, Dave Beneteau or Dan Severn, all of whom have lost their heads—and their matches—via the guillotine at the Ultimate Fighting Championship. Yet, like any technique, there is an antidote, and you can learn to defend against and escape from the guillotine against any opponent, regardless of his size or strength.

In Brazilian *jujutsu*, students are first taught the defensive aspects of fighting before they are allowed to progress to the strikes, throws, joint locks and choking techniques of the style. When in the proper defensive position, the jujutsu practitioner is not only safe from a larger, stronger opponent, but he also can effectively apply the deadly finishing moves for which the system is noted.

Pedro Sauer, who operates a Brazilian-jujutsu academy in Salt Lake City, learned early on from his instructor, the talented Rickson Gracie, that technique, not strength, is the secret to his system. According to Sauer, the best way to defend yourself from a guillotine choke is, of course, to prevent it from being applied. When shooting in, Sauer advises you to always protect

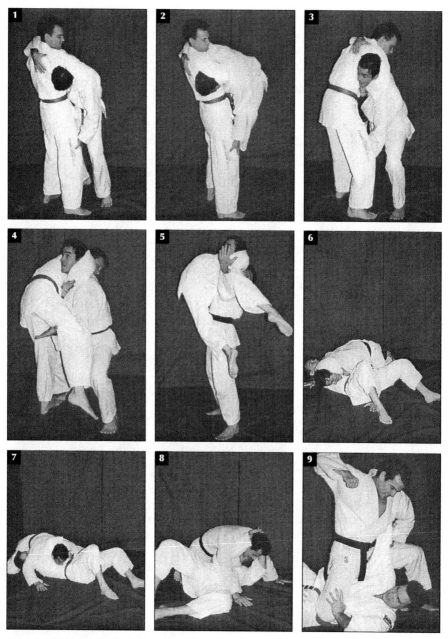

If caught (1) in a standing guillotine choke, clinch the attacker's shoulder and jump up (2), hooking the inside of the opponent's legs with your feet. It fatigues your opponent to have to hold your weight, and when you land, you can reach under (3) your adversary and force him to bend over. Keep your back straight and scoop up (4) your foe, lifting him (5) into position to slam back-first to the ground. Once the opponent is on the ground, assume (6) a cross-body position on top of him and, while maintaining a balanced foundation, circle (7-8) your adversary until you are able to release your head from the hold. You should now be in good position to deliver strikes (9) from above.

your neck by tucking the side of your head against your forward shoulder. This will prevent the opponent from putting you in a front head lock. If he gets a hold around your neck and arm together, you will be in no great danger. Simply maintain a good clinch, look upward, and slide around to his back. You will find yourself in an excellent position to choke or take the opponent to the ground.

Although many reality-tournament competitors have made use of the guillotine, once caught in the choke themselves, few have demonstrated the ability to escape this highly effective hold.

"First, you have to survive," notes Sauer. "You have to be patient; don't be too aggressive. It's better to be a dog who is alive than a lion who is dead."

Sauer claims that the most common mistake fighters make when caught in a guillotine choke is to try to pull their head out of the hold, which will actually only make the choke tighter. The secret to defending against the guillotine choke is to prevent the opponent from maneuvering for the extension needed to force submission or unconsciousness.

To defend against an opponent's guillotine from a standing position, simply clinch your adversary over one shoulder, hold him closely and "hang" your weight on him so he can't get the proper separation for the choke. Your other hand can be used to grip the opponent's wrist to relieve pressure on your neck. When this defense is executed properly, you can literally be lifted off your feet without harm. Not only is the pressure from the choke eliminated, but your opponent must support your entire weight, which will cause him almost immediate fatigue.

Once you neutralize the opponent's guillotine choke, plan your escape from the hold. One escape measure—which was effectively demonstrated by UFC VII champ Marco Ruas against quarterfinal opponent Larry Cureton—is a throwing technique. After you grab your opponent behind the legs and flip him onto his back, you can finish him off with any number of strikes or submission holds. But because the guillotine choke can also be applied on the ground, it is critical that you don't allow yourself to be

To escape a guillotine choke while caught in an opponent's guard (1), clinch your adversary's shoulder with your right arm and hold his wrist with your left hand, forcing his left elbow in. Shift your weight forward and drive your shoulder into the opponent's neck (2) while maintaining a wide base with your legs. Then bring your legs together (3) and bounce up and down as you slide through the opponent's guard. Once you are free of the guard, assume (4) a cross-body position as you prepare to free your neck from the guillotine. Move your right arm around the opponent's head while you maintain a grip on his right wrist. Dig (5) your chin into the opponent's ribs as you circle around him while maintaining a wide, balanced base. As you control the opponent's right arm, slide (6) your head out of the choke and initiate a painful arm lock (7). Fall back (8) and complete the arm lock by squeezing your legs together and raising your hips, which hyperextends the opponent's elbow.

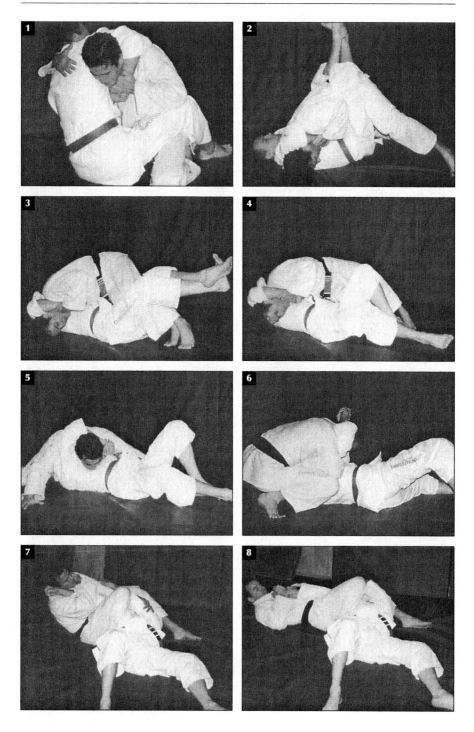

put in the guard position by your adversary. From the guard, the guillotine can be employed with optimum leverage.

To escape the guillotine choke while caught in the guard position, you must hold your opponent over his shoulder in the same manner as before and use your other hand to create some breathing room in the hold. Because of the additional leverage your adversary can apply with his legs while in this position, it is also important to push your weight forward and drive your shoulder into his neck.

When you begin your escape, you must remain as relaxed as possible. The tighter you are, the more difficult it will be to breathe and ultimately free yourself from the hold. Before removing your neck, however, you must first "pass" the opponent's guard position. This, too, should be accomplished in a calm, calculated manner while you maintain a solid foundation. The opponent will likely be so preoccupied with the guillotine choke that you will be able to slip through his legs in a slow, balanced, methodical manner. If you bring your legs slightly together, it will be even easier to slide out of his guard and into the cross-body position, where you can maneuver for a finishing hold.

The natural evolution of the martial arts has spawned not only new fighting techniques and strategies, but also effective defensive tactics to counter them. Understanding the dynamics of the guillotine choke and the proper way to escape from the hold will make you a more complete fighter and could someday literally save your neck.

MODIFYING BRAZILIAN JUJUTSU FOR THE NO-HOLDS-BARRED WORLD OF VALE TUDO

by Robert W. Young • Photos by Robert W. Young • February 1998

After the recent losses that practitioners of Brazilian *jujutsu* have experienced in mixed-martial arts events like the Ultimate Fighting Championship, a lot of people are beginning to think the art isn't all it was cracked up to be. They're saying that whenever a practitioner relies on only locks and chokes, he neglects a very important weapon—striking. They're also saying that Brazilian jujutsu loses some 70 percent of its techniques when it's practiced without a *gi*.

Well, these naysayers seem to be basing their assessments on some widespread misconceptions, says Pedro Carvalho, a Brazilian-jujutsu instructor based in Rancho Cucamonga, California. He says that in Brazil there exists a form of competition called *vale tudo*, which means "anything goes." It started as a kind of personal grudge match, but now the contests are held in a ring and a referee is present. Locks, throws, chokes, kicks and punches are all permitted, and no uniforms are worn. And Brazilian jujutsu is doing just fine there.

It's the open-ended nature of jujutsu that allows room for incorporating such diverse techniques, Carvalho says. His frequent training trips to Rio de Janeiro are the key to picking up the most up-to-date and effective grappling-striking combinations that can be used in a no-holds-barred fight—whether it takes place in the octagon or on the street.

The Facts

"Let me explain why we train primarily with a gi," Carvalho says. "When an instructor trains a new student, he uses a gi because without it, things are a lot harder. You have to be familiar with ground fighting with a gi before you try it standing, without a gi, as in vale tudo competition. It's a lot easier to learn the basics on the ground when you can grab the gi. But Brazilian jujutsu is very effective with or without a gi.

"In the beginning of no-holds-barred competitions in the United States, nobody stood a chance against Brazilian jujutsu. Now almost everybody—even boxers and kickboxers—trains in it. They study the art to learn how to defend against it. That means the jujutsu guys have a harder time, especially when there's a big size and weight difference."

Does being good in tournament jujutsu necessarily mean a martial artist is good in vale tudo? "Not necessarily," Carvalho says. "Not everybody in Brazil learns all three aspects of jujutsu: fighting with the gi, or tournament jujutsu;

 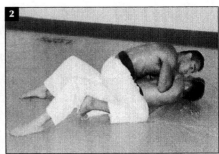

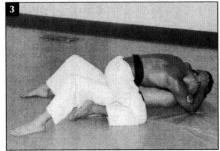 

From the mount, Pedro Carvalho forces his opponent to block his punches (1). He then pushes one arm to the side and slips his free arm around the opponent's neck (2). If the choke does not work (3), Carvalho can safely blast away at the ribs while keeping the arm trapped (4). He finishes with a choke executed from the side (5).

fighting without the gi, which is vale tudo; and self-defense, where a guy tries to punch you and you have to take him down and get away. Most instructors are not teaching all three aspects; most are teaching one or two."

And there are plenty of differences involved. "When tournament guys who are used to wearing a gi enter a vale tudo competition, they feel a little lost," Carvalho says. "A lot of techniques don't work well when you're sweaty. For example, with a gi you're taught to go for an armbar when you're in the mount position. Without a gi, you shouldn't because you and your opponent are too slippery. You should concentrate on staying in the top position and trying to finish the guy with a choke or knockout."

The following five sequences, derived from basic Brazilian-jujutsu techniques, have been battle-tested in Brazil's vale tudo arena. All incorporate simple strikes, and none depends on wearing a gi.

Sequence No. 1

Start in the mount position, from which you can punch your opponent at will. Of course, he'll try to protect his face with his hands and arms. "As soon as he does that, you must get his left arm out of the way by pushing it across his neck," Carvalho says. "Then you put your head down to hold it there and circle your left arm under his neck. Your left hand grabs your right biceps. Your right hand goes on the back of your neck. When you apply the pressure, it can cut off his blood and air supply."

If the choke does not work for some reason, let go with your right arm while continuing to pin his left arm against his neck. That frees your right arm to pummel his unprotected rib area. After a little softening up, hop over his torso and choke him from a different angle.

Sequence No. 2

Again, mount your opponent and try to punch him. One of his defensive options is to wrap his arms around your lower back and pull his head close to your chest. That leaves only the top of his head open to your downward-angled blows, and it would take only one or two of those to break the smaller

After achieving the mount, Carvalho again uses punches to make his opponent react (1). To avoid the blows, the opponent hugs Carvalho's torso (2). Carvalho circles his arm behind the opponent's neck and under his arm (3). To finish, he moves to the side and puts pressure on the neck (4).

bones in your hands. If you wish to continue striking, try using an elbow to the back of his neck.

"Some people can take a lot of punishment from this position and still not give up," Carvalho says. That hugging position, which your opponent thinks is safe, really offers you the chance to take him by surprise and effect a quick submission.

You need to lean forward and position your right arm so your armpit is behind your opponent's head, then move the same arm until it hooks high on his left arm. Make sure your right palm is flat on the mat. Next, abandon the mount by moving your body off to his right side. "Spread your legs for balance and keep your body straight up," Carvalho says.

It's important to maintain control of his right arm, which should still be wrapped around your waist. Grabbing the wrist ensures that it won't be yanked away. As you lean backward, apply pressure on his neck. "Be careful, because if you go all the way, you can break the guy's neck," Carvalho

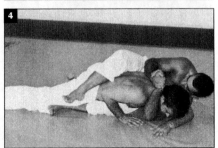
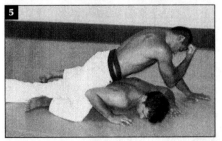

With his opponent held in his guard, Carvalho traps one arm and blocks punches from the other (1). He quickly encircles his neck (2), then locks his legs and executes a choke (3). If the choke fails, Carvalho can move to the opponent's back (4) and unload elbow strikes to the head (5).

says. "Always go slow so he has a chance to tap."

Sequence No. 3

If you have your opponent's back and are trying for a choke, he may be at a loss for an escape. When he starts getting desperate, he may try to get out of the hold by putting his right arm under your right leg so he can sneak out that way. That's when you need to place your left foot on his left hip and push so your hips move higher on his body. "Your right leg bends around his neck, and your left hand grabs your left ankle," Carvalho says. "Pull your ankle so you can hook it behind your left knee."

In a position that is really a reverse triangle choke, you have your opponent's neck and arm trapped between your legs. "When he raises his arm, you trap that, too," Carvalho says. You can even secure it by jamming it under your left armpit.

"At this point, you can strike him with your elbow," Carvalho says. "Or you can use one of several finishing techniques. You can lock his trapped arm until he taps, you can just sit forward and choke him out, or you can lie backward and push his head forward with both your arms."

Sequence No. 4

Another position in which you might find yourself is the bottom of a side head lock. While this might have presented a problem when you roamed the elementary-school playground, it's not too serious for anyone trained in Brazilian jujutsu or vale tudo competition.

First, use your left forearm to push upward on your opponent's neck. Then slide your left leg over his left leg and hook it around his thigh if you can; this provides the anchor with which you will move your body to his back.

Once you're on top, place your palms on the mat and use your left elbow to pin his head down. Then complete the transition to the mount. If you want, you can deliver a few punches to the exposed ribs on his right side. The finishing technique involves locking down his shoulder and head with your left arm and using your neck to lift his trapped right arm. Because you have secured your base on top of his body, he cannot roll out of the hold.

Sequence No. 5

Once again, your opponent is in your guard. He tries to punch you while he's between your legs, which happens fairly often in vale tudo and mixed-martial arts competition. You respond by blocking the punches and grabbing his upper arms to prevent any more attacks.

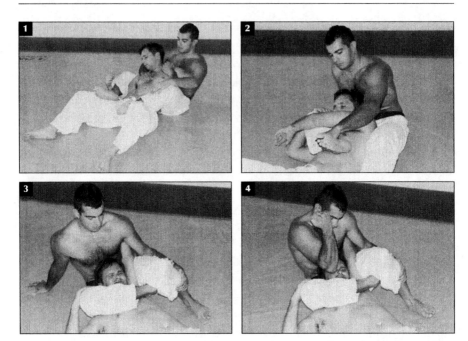

Carvalho attempts a rear-naked choke, and his opponent tries to escape by reaching under Carvalho's leg (1). Carvalho moves toward the opponent's head and wraps his leg around his neck (2). He then executes a reverse triangle choke with an armbar (3). At the same time, he can deliver an elbow strike to the face (4).

Next, move your left shin to your opponent's right armpit so you can push his arm away. Holding his right triceps temporarily immobilizes that limb. You then pull him toward your chest and trap his neck and left arm with your own left arm. Your head helps secure his left arm. From this position, you can choke him using the technique discussed in the first sequence.

"To finish him, you've got to get your arm against his throat and trap his arm at the same time," Carvalho says. "If he keeps his chin down, that can be very difficult to do."

If the choke fails and your opponent tries to stand and escape, maintain your grip around his neck and transfer your left foot to his right knee. "Then you push his knee to flatten him and keep him from standing," Carvalho says. "Your right foot goes over his body, and you end up on his back."

If your opponent stays flat on his stomach and you have a hard time hooking your other foot under his thigh (which you probably will want to do to increase your stability there), switch to a punch or elbow strike.

"Avoid punching his head, because you can break your hand," Carvalho says. "As soon as you hit his neck with your elbow, he will lift his head. Then it will be easier to choke him."

Closing Thoughts

For martial artists accustomed only to tournament-oriented grappling matches, the possibility of hitting and being hit can dramatically change the way you attack and defend. "Sometimes you're in a position where you just want to defend yourself," Carvalho says. "Other times you just want to get away. For example, if the guy starts to choke you or joint-lock you, why should you try to hit him? You should try to get out first. Then you can get in a safe position and hit him or use a finishing technique. If you try to strike when you're in danger, you might get tired. Then you'll be in more trouble, and you'll have wasted precious time."

Whenever you're in the mount, make sure your knees are close to your opponent's armpits. "If you mount him too low, he can thrust his hips upward and throw you off," says Carvalho.

He also cautions that the guard, although an undeniably strong position in jujutsu tournaments, can be bad business in a street fight. "You shouldn't put your opponent in your guard on purpose," Carvalho says. "A good jujutsu fighter ends up there only if his opponent puts him there. If things go that way, there are a lot of tools that work from the guard, but you should never choose to have your back on the asphalt."

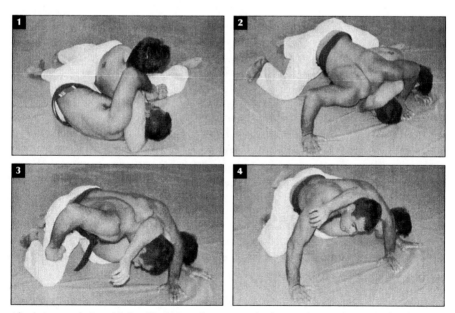

After being caught in a side head lock, Carvalho positions his leg over his opponent's thigh and uses his arm to push against his neck (1). He then circles to the opponent's back (2). Because he maintains control of the opponent's arm and head, he can easily punch the ribs (3). Carvalho finishes by applying upward pressure on the trapped arm (4).

WHICH STYLE WORKS BEST IN MIXED-MARTIAL ARTS COMPETITION?
The Stats Are In!
It's Wrestling, America's Martial Art

by Christopher A. Colderley • Photo by Fernando Escovar • November 1998

In his 1986 book *Western Boxing and World Wrestling*, John Gilbey contemplated how well different wrestling systems might fare in mixed-martial arts competitions. Although he noted the difficulty of changing styles for the practitioners of almost any discipline, he sided with the martial arts, particularly *jujutsu*.

Gilbey closed with a quote from Higashi, a Japanese jujutsu expert who in 1905 spoke about the subject of wrestling verses jujutsu: "American wrestlers are strong—much stronger than any of us pretend to be in muscular strength. After all, however, wrestling is wrestling. Against jujutsu, it is mere child's play. I have met a number of Western wrestlers, and they are as helpless as babes against jujutsu. And no one versed in the art of jujutsu is mad enough to expect anything else."

Many of these suspicions seem to have been confirmed in recent mixed-martial arts competitions. Since the first Ultimate Fighting Championship in 1993, Brazilian jujutsu has achieved a certain fame in the mixed-martial arts community. Royce Gracie used this discipline to win three events (UFC I, II and IV) and draw in a 35-minute superfight with Ken Shamrock in UFC V. Other Brazilian martial artists also contributed to the prominence of jujutsu: Renzo and Ralph Gracie in the World Combat Championship and Extreme Fighting I, II, III and IV, respectively; Vitor Belfort in UFC XII and XIII; and Marcus "Conan" Silveira in Extreme Fighting I and II.

In fact, these Brazilian-jujutsu stylists were so dominant at times that some observers contemplated whether they could ever be beaten. The impact of Brazilian fighters on the martial arts has been enormous. *Black Belt*'s Robert W. Young noted: "They have almost single-handedly forced the martial arts community to open its eyes with regard to the effectiveness of ground fighting. Thanks to them, a large percentage of martial arts schools in this country now advertise instruction in jujutsu, wrestling, judo or simply grappling." Given the profile of jujutsu fighters in mixed-martial arts events, the attention devoted to this style seems warranted.

Statistics Don't Lie

When the overall record is considered, however, the success of Brazilian jujutsu is somewhat questionable. Table I, for example, ranks jujutsu as the No. 2 style, with a record of 29-20-1, behind wrestling (44-21) and ahead of shootfighting (26-9-2). Moreover, Table II, which displays the winning percentages of various styles with at least 10 decisions, shows that jujutsu (59.2 percent) is much more successful than boxing, karate, kickboxing and kung fu, but it ranks behind shootfighting, *sambo* and wrestling, and it is only slightly ahead of pit fighting in terms of success in the octagon.

Table III shows how well different disciplines have fared in tournament finals, superfights and championship matches. Grappling styles, such as wrestling, shootfighting and jujutsu, are by far the most successful. American wrestlers, however, have dominated the tournaments, winning 11 finals, three superfights and two heavyweight championship bouts. Jujutsu, by contrast, has won only four tournament championships and is 6-5 in these events overall.

The Art or the Artist?

Perhaps a more telling indication of wrestling's dominance in mixed-martial arts matches comes from a review of the 14 "winningest" fighters. These fighters are among the most successful in these competitions and have proved their ability in many high-level matches. By focusing specifically on them, the trap of including the records of less-experienced and less-qualified fighters is avoided.

As Table IV illustrates, grappling arts such as wrestling, shootfighting and jujutsu are among the most successful. Wrestling, however, is represented most often with five fighters in the top 10, ranking second, third, fifth and two at ninth. Jujutsu, by contrast, has only two fighters in the top 14, one ranking first and the other 10th. The success of several wrestlers supports the notion that wrestling is an effective method for use in reality-based events.

Finally, by examining the results from finals, championships and superfights that pitted wrestling against jujutsu (shown in Table V), it can be determined that wrestling has a 3-1 record against jujutsu.

Royce Gracie, the Anomaly

Brazilian-jujutsu expert Royce Gracie has achieved legendary status based on his tournament victories and remains the only undefeated fighter in the UFC (with more than five victories).

However, Gracie has not competed since UFC V, and many are skeptical of his early success against unknowing opponents. For example, Kathy

Long, a former kickboxing champion who now boxes professionally, said: "When the UFC started, the promoters claimed they were going to pit martial artists of different styles against each other. The individuals who represented the martial arts in the early UFCs were not up to par. So to have such an event serve as a showcase is ridiculous."

Don "The Dragon" Wilson concurred: "There was only one person in the beginning who had experience at that type of fighting, and that was Royce Gracie. And, of course, that's why he won the first show so quickly and easily. But as it went on and fighters got experience, all of a sudden he was having draws and had to bow out one time [owing to fatigue]. He had the edge in the very beginning, but at this point, there are no secrets

Wrestling champion Mark Kerr has a 4-0 record in mixed-martial arts competition.

to this style of competition."

Frank Shamrock, the current middleweight champion of the UFC, said: "No one knew anything about grappling when he was fighting. He caught everyone by surprise. Everyone is much more knowledgeable now, and I don't believe he would enjoy the same success."

Shootfighting Rules!

Overall, shootfighters—who employ a range of striking, grappling and submission tactics—are the most successful competitors in mixed-martial arts events when ranked by percentage. For example, shootfighting is second only to wrestling in total wins in championship and superfight matches, and two shootfighters rank in the top 14 fighters. It is the most successful style in championships and superfights, where it has achieved a record of 5-1 against wrestling and 2-0 against Brazilian jujutsu.

It is interesting to note that most of these top fighters are associated with Ken Shamrock's Lion's Den school and have experience in combat grappling. Their system has benefited substantially from the collaboration of many different martial artists, including Ken Shamrock, Frank Shamrock and former UFC and heavyweight kickboxing champion Maurice Smith. Throughout its evolution in the UFC, shootfighting has committed itself to developing counters and strategies against Brazilian jujutsu and wrestling.

Wrestling's Winning Ways

Why have wrestlers fared so well against jujutsu in UFC-type competition? A variety of factors might account for this success. First, wrestlers have been able to counter the numerous takedowns employed by Brazilian-jujutsu practitioners. Not only are wrestlers highly trained and skilled in diverting shoots and throws, but they also have the ability to employ takedowns and can use them to neutralize their opponents.

Second, the rules of the UFC have tended to favor wrestling more than jujutsu. The fact that wrestlers do not have to wear a uniform greatly assists them against martial artists. Wrestlers are used to employing takedowns without the benefit of a uniform or belt to grab, while many jujutsu tactics rely on the use of the uniform. (Some commentators have estimated that Brazilian jujutsu loses about 70 percent of its techniques when uniforms are not worn.)

Third, many Brazilian-jujutsu practitioners oppose the use of time limits. One popular tactic of theirs is to employ the guard to protect themselves and wait until their opponent has tired sufficiently to apply a submission hold. In Brazilian competitions, for example, there are accounts of some fights lasting more than three hours. Hence, when matches are only 10 or 15 minutes long, wrestlers can more easily control their jujutsu opponents without tiring.

Fourth, the use of the fence is opposed by most Brazilian-jujutsu stylists, who believe that it allows their opponent to avoid being taken down and to gain leverage against submissions and reversals. Wrestlers who have trained for mixed-martial arts competitions are well aware of the advantages of the fence and use this as a tactic, whereas most Brazilian-jujutsu practitioners do not train with the fence in mind because *vale tudo* matches are held in a ring. Carlson Gracie and Mario Sperry have said they oppose the use of the fence because it prevents Brazilian-jujutsu fighters from displaying their full range of skills and techniques.

No Respect

The UFC was initially developed to determine what works and what doesn't. Such events have proved—almost conclusively—that grappling styles have a better rate of success than do purely striking and stand-up styles. In spite of the accomplishment of wrestling in NHB events, many modern jujutsu practitioners hold a general disdain for American wrestling—just as Higashi did.

Rickson Gracie, for example, said: "You see big, strong wrestlers in these events who can control people, but they have not learned finishing holds. So to win their fights, they control and smash their opponent, which is different from locking, choking or subduing someone with clean techniques. The wrestlers can't finish their opponent in a skilled, smooth manner, so the fights get ugly."

If jujutsu is really superior to the techniques of the big, strong but unskilled wrestlers, it has not yet demonstrated it in mixed-martial arts events—with the exception of Royce Gracie's early UFC matches.

Clear Conclusion

Throughout the history of the martial arts, the challenge match was used as a way of promoting different fighting systems and determining what worked and what didn't. Although mixed-martial arts events are an imperfect imitation of reality, they are the best alternative available for assessing different arts, and the effectiveness of the various arts must be judged from the available empirical evidence.

Even though successful fighters must rely on a mix of systems, the evidence indicates that wrestling provides a good base for mixed-martial arts competitions. Wrestlers can neutralize strikes by using shooting techniques to counter their opponents, and they can fight competently on the ground, where most fights end. They also have excellent strength and conditioning.

Based on its accomplishments in the UFC and other MMA events, wrestling provides an effective—but not necessarily superior—foundation for fighting and self-defense against any type of opponent. In the words of David "Tank" Abbott at UFC XII, wrestling is truly "America's martial art."

Table I: Top Three Styles in the UFC

Rank	Style	Wins	Losses	Draws
1	Wrestling	44	21	0
2	Jujutsu	29	20	1
3	Shootfighting	26	9	2

(Source: UFC, Ultimate Fighters)

Table II: UFC Records and Winning Percentages of Styles

Style	Wins	Losses	Draws	Win Percentage
Shootfighting	26	9	2	74.3%
Sambo	7	3	1	70.0%
Wrestling	44	21	0	67.7%
Jujutsu	29	20	1	59.2%
Pit fighting	11	8	0	57.9%
Boxing	3	5	0	37.5%
Kickboxing	13	24	0	35.1%
Karate	10	22	0	31.3%
Kung Fu	4	12	0	25.0%

(Source: UFC, Ultimate Fighters)

Table III: Victories in Tournament Finals, Superfights and Championships

Style	Tournaments	Superfights	Championships	Wins	Losses
Wrestling	11	3	2	16	11
Brazilian Jujutsu	4	2	0	6	5
Shootfighting	3	5	2	10	1
Sambo	1	0	0	1	1
Vale Tudo	1	0	0	1	0
Kickboxing	0	0	2	2	1
Ninjutsu	1	0	0	1	0

(Source: UFC, Ultimate Fighters)

Table IV: Top 14 Fighters, by Wins

Fighter	Style	Wins	Losses	Draws	Percentage
Royce Gracie	Brazilian Jujutsu	11	0	1	100.0%
Don Frye	Wrestling	9	1	0	90.0%
Dan Severn	Wrestling	9	3	0	75.0%
David Abbott	Pit Fighting	8	6	0	57.1%
Mark Coleman	Wrestling	6	2	0	75.0%
Ken Shamrock	Shootfighting	6	2	2	75.0%
Oleg Taktarov	Sambo	6	2	1	75.0%
Jerry Bohlander	Shootfighting	5	1	0	83.3%
Randy Couture	Wrestling	4	0	0	100.0%
Mark Kerr	Wrestling	4	0	0	100.0%
Guy Mezger	Kickboxing	4	0	0	100.0%
Vitor Belfort	Brazilian Jujutsu	4	1	0	80.0%
Marco Ruas	Vale Tudo	4	1	0	80.0%
Pat Smith	Kickboxing	4	2	0	66.7%

(Source: UFC, Ultimate Fighters)

Table V: Head-to-Head in Finals, Superfights and Championships

	Wrestling	B.J.J.	Shootfighting	Kickboxing	Pit Fighting	Wins
Wrestling	---	3	1	1	1	6
Brazilian Jujutsu	1	---	0	2	2	5
Shootfighting	5	2	---	0	0	7
Kickboxing	1	0	0	---	1	2
Pit Fighting	0	0	0	0	---	0
Losses	7	5	1	3	4	---

NO-HOLDS-BARRED CHAMP BAS RUTTEN:
The Dutch Star of Japan's Pancrase Circuit Is Making His American Debut in the UFC

by Jake Rossen • Photos by Robert W. Young • April 1999

There is a certain grace to Bas Rutten's fighting, a flurry of movement working toward a singular goal: to hurt, to stun, to surprise, to win. He hits with the force of a jackhammer and torques submissions to effect maximum loss of will. Since an eye-opening loss to Ken Shamrock four years ago, there has not been a time in more than 20 fights when Rutten's hand was not raised in victory.

If American fight fans don't know Rutten's name by now, they will come January 1999, when the Dutch fighter makes his long-awaited debut in the Ultimate Fighting Championship. A star in Japan's Pancrase events for years, Rutten is itching for exposure on the other side of the ocean. After beating the likes of Frank Shamrock and Maurice Smith, it is a journey he's well prepared for.

Entering the Ring

But will the rule structure of the UFC throw Rutten off? Getting mounted in a Pancrase match, for example, leaves you vulnerable to submissions but rarely to strikes. "I'm not a stupid fighter," Rutten says. "I train for that, too. In Pancrase, [striking] is allowed, only they don't do it. When somebody starts hitting you, you're going to hit back. It's pretty much the same. It's really difficult to hit somebody with a clear shot on the ground."

Rutten's first UFC opponent is likely to be Tsuyoshi Kohsaka, a solid fighter with a 2-0 record in the octagon. "Kohsaka is already a very good fighter," Rutten says. "He has good ground submissions, and his striking is getting better. He's training with Maurice Smith. It's going to be a tough fight. He knows my game. I will try to strike, to see if my strikes go through, and on the ground I will do my work."

Rutten was originally supposed to fight Randy Couture in the UFC Brazil in October of 1998, but it never came together. "Randy pulled out for money reasons," Rutten explains. "I pulled out later, also for money reasons. They said that it was going to be on pay-per-view, that I was going to fight Randy Couture for the title. And then they said, 'We have to pay you less money.' That's OK, you know, because still I can fight for the title. But then Randy pulled out."

Couture recently suffered his first loss in Japan against Enson Inoue, and Rutten isn't surprised. "I think I could have defeated him, also," he says. "I trained with the best wrestlers in the world. I trained with the guy who beat him six times in Greco-Roman wrestling [Darrel Gholar]."

Rutten respects wrestlers but doesn't hand anything to them. "They're really good at taking somebody down, but they don't have the finishing holds," he says. "You can't learn that in six months. Nobody can."

When quizzed about who the best fighter out there may be, Rutten pauses before compiling his list. "I think Frank Shamrock's really good," he says. "Mark Kerr, Marco Ruas, Pedro Rizzo. I've got to put myself in the line, too. But being good in striking, punching, kicking and grappling does not mean you can't get caught with a lucky punch. Anything can happen."

The Skills

Even though Rutten is well-versed in submissions, he's known mainly as a devastating striker. Asked if it bothers him, he sighs: "Yeah, but that's OK. A lot of people don't know. They forget that about 70 percent of my opponents I finish with submission holds. When I strike somebody, I break his liver or break his ribs. Then people say, 'Wow, he's a good striker!' "

Good striker that he is, Rutten still comes under fire for his Pancrase background, where more rules are in place and closed-fist punches to the head are prohibited. But he's undaunted by the complaints. "I can hit with my fists now," he says. "People don't understand, but when you have to hit with palm strikes, it's much more difficult. It takes away your speed, your accuracy—everything. So once I can hit with my fists, it's going to be better."

Rutten will also be unhindered by the Pancrase regulation gear. "Striking without my knee pads and shin protection … normally, I have to hit somebody five times with a kick. Now it's going to be two times or one time."

Rutten is also aware that the venue change might seem odd to a fighter used to the silent crowds in Japan. "[In America] everybody's screaming at the top of their lungs. 'Give him a right punch, give him a left hook, give him an armbar.' In Japan, everybody knows that the fighter knows what to do. Everybody's quiet. It's really strange. I can talk with the guy all the way upstairs in the last row—from the ring! It's so quiet in Japan. They respect everybody who steps into the ring."

Rutten believes that most Westerners aren't aware of what races through a fighter's mind before an event. "People don't realize what it is to walk into a ring and fight," he says. "Your family is around you, your friends are there, people are watching. It's a lot of pressure."

Déjà Vu

The aforementioned wins over Shamrock and Smith will provide a nice backdrop for upcoming fights between Rutten and either man. Rutten feels confident that he can make history repeat itself, though he realizes Shamrock, in particular, has improved with time. "He definitely did," Rutten admits. "But it's the same with me, you know. People say, 'You fought him [a long time ago].' I don't stop learning, either."

Anticipating Smith's upcoming return to the octagon, Rutten likes the idea of a rematch. "If he wants to come back, we're probably going to meet each other again," he says. "It's going to be the third time. It's going to be fun."

On the UFC

Earlier UFC fights were sometimes noted for their lengthy stalls, but Rutten likes to end his matches quickly. "When you're a really good submission fighter, you can finish somebody within two minutes," he says. "When you say that you're the best, you should finish him within two minutes. When they break you up after five minutes, don't say, 'Yeah, I was just working my way.' You know the referee is going to stand you up, so you have to work a little bit harder."

Asked about the reason for the popularity of freestyle fighting, Rutten is blunt. "I think everybody likes to fight," he says. "At a certain age, most people find out it's not for them, so they choose something else. But deep in their heart, every guy likes to fight."

Yet much of the fighting that takes place in mixed-martial arts matches is misunderstood by the audience. "Even now I can tell that people don't know what a leg lock is," he says. "Pro wrestlers really show things, and people think, 'I got my money's worth there.' But with submission, you can get caught in a leg lock that's really not exciting, but at that moment, it can break your leg or your knee. It's the same with armbars and chokes. They don't look spectacular. Only the people who really know what's going on—who have felt it in training—know it's real."

Looking Ahead

Rutten is optimistic about the future of the sport of no-holds-barred fighting. "Very big," he says. "It's a release for aggression for people who watch it. It's better to watch a bout than it is to fight in the street. That's what every sport does, especially martial arts.

"My brother's a lawyer. His wife went to a Thai boxing fight of mine.

She watched it in the beginning, and they were almost walking out of the place. But at the end, they were screaming at the top of their lungs, 'Kick his head off!' Afterward, they said they felt a release, they felt so good. All their anger was out."

Rutten is confident that he can enjoy as much success in the UFC as he did in Thai boxing and Pancrase events. Where will he be in five years? "In the movies," he predicts. "And, I hope, still undefeated."

Top-10 Techniques of Pancrase

Bas Rutten, a three-time King of Pancrase, has been practicing the hybrid art of Pancrase for a measly five years, but that training and his decade-long background in *muay Thai* (he was ranked fifth in the world) and karate (with second-degree black belts in *kyokushin* and *taekwondo*) have permitted him to quickly rise to the top. The following are the top 10 techniques Rutten used when he competed in Pancrase.

Low Roundhouse

The low roundhouse kick to the legs is one of Rutten's most powerful techniques. Like muay Thai kickboxers, he likes to strike with his shin. "You can use it to hit the inside or outside of your opponent's thigh," he

Low Roundhouse

says. "You can also attack his body, but it is usually more protected and harder to reach."

Rutten advises martial artists to always kick with 100-percent commitment, even if your opponent raises his shin to block your kick, as Thai boxers do. Never use a soft kick as a feint to open him up for a second technique, he says, because that can give a crafty opponent all the time he needs to enter, clinch and take you down.

High Roundhouse

Grapplers tend to keep their hands low when they close the distance for a takedown. That's why Rutten recommends using a high roundhouse kick aimed at a relatively unprotected body part—the head. Contrary to what some martial artists say about the dangers of attempting a head kick, Rutten says it can be more dangerous to try a body kick: "If you kick to the grappler's body, he'll grab your leg and throw you to the ground."

Rutten prefers to use the shin when striking high because it possesses knockout power and does not risk injury to the bones, ligaments and muscles on top of the foot. If, however, you are wearing shoes or instep protectors, it's OK to kick with the foot, he says.

High Roundhouse

Rear Cross

Rear Cross

"In Pancrase, you can't punch with a closed fist," Rutten says. "But I've still had knockouts with the rear cross—using the palm." That's because the rear cross draws its power from the twisting of the body and transmits that power to the striking surface via the punching arm. It's the power of the twist that matters, not the hardness of the striking surface.

The open-hand-striking rule of Pancrase is necessary because fighters compete an average of 10 times a year and do not have the luxury of long recovery periods between matches, Rutten claims. On the street, however, you need not worry about your attacker's recovery time, so go ahead and close that fist if you think your wrist and knuckles can withstand the force.

Body Punch

"Whenever you strike the body of your opponent, of course you want to use your fists," Rutten says. "I come from kyokushin karate, so my body punches have always been good." Virtually any style of karate can provide you with an equally good base for body punching.

Martial artists tend to drive their punches horizontally into their

Body Punch

opponent's body, but Rutten prefers to throw his at an angle. "I like to push the ribs upward," he says. "The liver is a good target, but it's a little behind the ribs, so you have to push up to get it. The solar plexus is another good target because a solid blow can knock the wind out of anybody."

Knee Thrust

Rutten has knocked out four opponents with the knee thrust. For decades, Thai boxers have found the simple technique just as effective. "It's one of my favorite weapons because the legs are the strongest part of the body," he says.

"You can use the knee to strike your opponent's head, body or legs," Rutten says. "You can even use it to strike while you're on the ground. No matter how you do it, it can be very painful."

Knee Thrust

Heel Hook

The heel hook was one of the first grappling techniques Rutten learned for the ring. Now he swears by it. "It's very dangerous," he says. "I broke the shinbone of a Japanese guy with it."

Twisting the heel puts pressure on three areas of the opponent's leg—the kneecap, shinbone and ankle—and can do serious damage to any or all of them. "In Pancrase in Japan, it's not allowed anymore," Rutten says. "During the first year I was there, 12 people were injured by it." Of course, that doesn't mean you can't use it in self-defense.

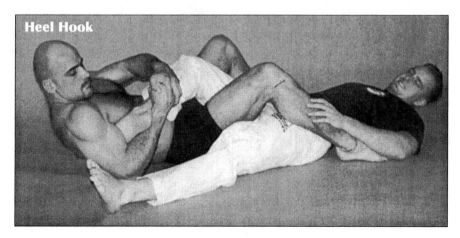

Heel Hook

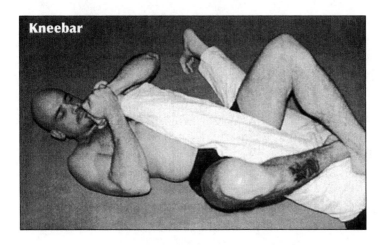

Kneebar

"You can do the kneebar from a lot of positions," Rutten says. "You can do it standing up or on the ground. Once you get it locked on, it can break your opponent's knee."

Ankle Hold

After trapping the opponent's lower leg against your chest, be sure to arch your back and push your hips forward to achieve maximum effect, Rutten says. You can do a lot of damage to your partner, so always use caution while practicing this technique.

Ankle Hold

The ankle hold can be done from almost any position—on the top or on the bottom. Just grab the blade of your opponent's foot with your opposite hand (i.e., use your right hand to grab his left foot or vice versa), slip your other arm under his ankle and lock that hand onto your opposite wrist. Then twist till he taps.

Side Choke

Rutten has used the side choke to render opponents unconscious in competition, so you can rest assured that it really works. "It puts pressure on the neck and cuts off the blood supply to the brain," he says.

To do it, put your upper body on your opponent's chest, leaving your legs spread wide on the ground to act as a base. "Then you push his arm across his neck—until it's next to your head," he says.

With your arm pinching the arteries on one side of his neck and his own arm pinching the arteries on the other side, it's lights out for him.

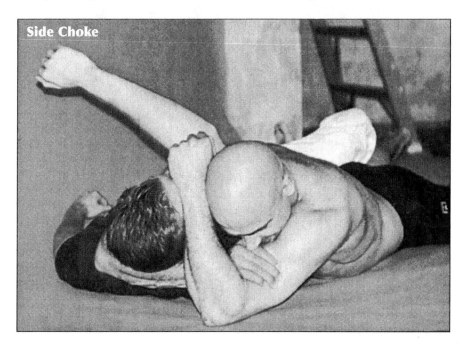
Side Choke

Triangle Choke

Most martial artists have seen the triangle choke performed against an opponent held in the guard, but it also functions against an opponent you have mounted. "If you really don't like him, you don't choke him out with your legs; you use your legs to hold him while you punch," Rutten says.

If you would rather use the technique to choke, remember that the principle is the same as for the side choke: Your opponent's arm constricts the blood flow on one side of his neck, and your your leg constricts the flow on the other. For best results, keep his arm across the front of his neck and pull his head forward.

Triangle Choke

RISE AND FALL OF WRESTLING
Three Methods for Resurrecting the Winning Ways of the Grappling Art

by Christopher A. Colderley • April 2000

The success of grappling in mixed-martial arts competition has been documented since the first Ultimate Fighting Championship was held in 1992. Much of the attention has been devoted to Brazilian *jujutsu*, based largely on the early performances of Royce Gracie in the UFC. However, practitioners of freestyle and Greco-Roman wrestling—including Dan Severn, Mark Coleman, Randy Couture, Mark Kerr and Kevin Jackson—have also amassed numerous accolades in MMA events.

The achievements of wrestlers in MMA events, however, have been overshadowed since Coleman lost the UFC XIV heavyweight championship on July 27, 1997. Until that fight, many followers of MMA competition thought Coleman was unstoppable. He had accumulated a record of 6-0 and finished many of his opponents within minutes, but his seeming invincibility ended that night with a unanimous decision to kickboxer Maurice Smith.

Striker's Revenge

More than any other, the Coleman-Smith fight signaled a change in the MMA hierarchy. No longer could wrestlers be content to simply take down their opponents and pound them into submission. Ground fighting had evolved sufficiently to allow strikers to defend themselves on the mat and even to execute some timely strikes or submissions. Even if the striker could not apply a finishing hold, a few basic ground techniques could allow him to defend himself against a downward attack until he could escape or neutralize his opponent long enough for the referee to restart the action.

Since the Coleman-Smith fight, several other prominent wrestlers have lost in MMA events. The highly touted Royce Alger, a two-time NCAA champion and two-time World Cup winner, succumbed to an armbar from *shooto* fighter Enson Inoue at UFC XIII, as did Couture at a recent event in Japan. Jackson was submitted by Frank Shamrock in seconds at Ultimate Japan and defeated in the UFC XVI superfight by Jerry Bohlander. More recently, Kevin Randleman lost a split decision to Bas Rutten at UFC XX after controlling his opponent on the ground for virtually the entire match.

The lesson seems clear: Wrestlers can no longer rely solely on their takedowns and ground skills to carry them through a fight. To compete at high levels in MMA competition, they must adapt their skills and techniques.

The history of wrestling in MMA events shows how the MMA community has adapted to the techniques of wrestlers. In a similar manner, wrestlers will have to adopt new techniques and strategies to improve their chances of victory.

Double-Leg Tackle

One technique wrestlers rely on too often is the double-leg tackle. A wrestler can execute this standard takedown while standing up to six feet away from his opponent by dropping and shooting in on the other man's legs. That allows the wrestler to stay out of striking range until there is an opening to exploit.

The wrestler can also execute the double-leg tackle while clinching with his opponent. When there's an opening, the wrestler simply steps between his opponent's legs, drops for the tackle and drives forward. If he encounters resistance, he can use his driving foot to step behind the opponent's heel and trip him.

There are two basic drawbacks to using this technique. First, even when it is properly executed, the opponent may choose to fall directly on his back and assume a guard position. This allows him to defend himself against strikes and wait for an opening to escape or apply a submission. Consider, for example, Frank Shamrock's championship match against Jackson at Ultimate Japan. Following Jackson's takedown, Frank Shamrock fell onto his back and positioned himself for an armbar.

Second, when the wrestler shoots in or drops down for the double-leg tackle, he may be vulnerable to a guillotine choke or a tie-up. In the UFC VI superfight between Ken Shamrock and Severn, this drawback became apparent when Severn left his neck exposed to the guillotine while trying to execute a tackle. Similarly, in Ultimate Brazil, Jeremy Horn was caught in a guillotine choke while shooting for Ebenezer Braga's legs.

If any doubt remains about the possible pitfalls of the double-leg tackle, consider the match between Gary Goodridge and wrestler Paul Herrera at UFC VIII. When Herrera attempted a tackle, Goodridge tied up his arms and landed several devastating elbows to the wrestler's jaw.

In addition to these dramatic examples, many other counters can be used against a double-leg tackle. For example, you can counter the technique by dropping to one knee and blocking the tackler's shoulder with an elbow. Likewise, a cross-face technique may be employed by grabbing the tackler's upper arm and forcing his head down and away from his body.

Ground and Pound

The expression "ground and pound" was coined to describe how Coleman subdues his opponents: a ferocious takedown combined with hammer-like downward strikes. Other prominent wrestlers such as Kerr, Severn and Dave Beneteau, as well as submission fighter Ken Shamrock, have used variations of this strategy to win in MMA events.

The effectiveness of the ground and pound was first brought into question during the UFC XIV heavyweight championship between Coleman and Smith. Despite his limited grappling experience, Smith neutralized Coleman's signature attack by skillfully using the guard to defend against the strikes. At times, Smith was even able to launch some devastating elbow strikes from his back. When the former kickboxing champ eventually escaped, he used punches and kicks to capture a unanimous decision over his exhausted opponent.

That match highlights the shortcoming of the ground and pound: A martial artist who is skilled at fighting from the guard can thwart downward strikes by controlling the wrestler's arms and using his legs to upset his balance when strikes are attempted. More important, the guard can be used to wear down the wrestler until an escape or submission presents itself. The effectiveness of the ground and pound is even more suspect with the prohibition of head butts in many MMA events.

Perhaps the best demonstration of what a skilled submission fighter can do against a wrestler occurred in the UFC IV match between Severn and Gracie. Despite being on his back for more than 15 minutes, Gracie defended against Severn's attack—which included head butts—until he could apply a triangle choke. Few who are familiar with Brazilian jujutsu and the skill of the Gracie system were surprised by this outcome, but many MMA observers were shocked that a wrestler could be choked out by someone on his back in a defensive position. Surely, that was one of the first signals that wrestling skills alone do not guarantee victory.

Revising the Stance

To make wrestlers more successful in MMA events, their basic stance must be modified. It is ordinarily a fairly upright position with the knees bent slightly, the hands held at waist level, the palms turned slightly downward and the weight evenly distributed on the feet. However, that stance leaves the wrestler vulnerable to kicks aimed at the legs and head. Coleman discovered that during UFC XIV, when Smith executed several devastating leg kicks that left Coleman severely bruised. And at UFC XVII, Pete Williams scored with some effective low kicks before landing a match-ending roundhouse kick to Coleman's face.

Defending against strikes is relatively simple and requires only a few adjustments to the basic wrestling stance. First, the hands must be raised to face-level so the wrestler can throw and protect against punches. Second, some weight must be shifted to the rear foot so the wrestler can evade an attack or respond with a leg block, which can cause severe damage to the opponent's shin. Third, the body must be turned slightly away from the opponent to decrease the exposure of the fighter's targets.

Although modifying the wrestling stance can reduce the effectiveness of certain takedowns, it provides needed protection against strikes. In Ultimate Japan, Couture used similar modifications to protect himself against the potent punching and kicking attacks of Smith. Eventually, Couture executed a takedown and controlled Smith on the mat—and won the heavyweight championship.

Reworking the Clinch

Even though many MMA fighters have learned basic counters to wrestling takedowns, wrestlers can easily modify their techniques for new attacks. One of the most basic—and devastating—techniques that can be added to a wrestling clinch is the *muay Thai* knee thrust. In UFC XV, Kerr demonstrated just how decisive the knee thrust can be when he knocked out hand-to-hand expert Greg Stott in 19 seconds. And in UFC XVII, Dan Henderson delivered successive knee blows by pulling down his opponent's head from the clinch.

Wrestlers can also employ a close-range technique called the "snap down." It requires them to place their hand on the back of their opponent's neck and sharply pull his head downward. That motion disturbs the opponent's balance and puts him in perfect position for a follow-up strike.

Rethinking the Ground

Unlike Brazilian jujutsu or Russian *sambo*, wrestling does not include sophisticated submission techniques. Finishing an opponent is complicated by the sophisticated use of the guard to tie up a wrestler and defend against his downward strikes. Wrestlers can draw on three techniques to overcome these obstacles. First, judo's bent-arm lock and straight-arm lock can be applied relatively easily on the ground, especially when the wrestler is stronger. Ideally, these techniques are best used from the side mount, but they can also be utilized effectively in the half-guard. In UFC XVII, Mike

Van Arsdale defeated Brazilian-jujutsu stylist Joe Pardo by applying a bent-arm lock from the side mount, marking one of the few times a wrestler has submitted a Brazilian-jujutsu practitioner in MMA combat.

Second, wrestlers can use the side mount to apply various chokes and cranks. For example, a cross-face choke, which is often used in wrestling to pin the opponent's shoulders, can secure a submission. In the first Ultimate Ultimate, Severn defeated the much larger Paul Varelans using this choke. And Coleman used it to defeat Severn in UFC XII.

Third, wrestlers can use the side mount or the basic head-control posi-

One drawback to using the double-leg tackle is that a skilled opponent can fall onto his back and pull you into his guard. To illustrate, Royce Gracie (left) faces Steve Neklia (1). Neklia shoots in and grabs Gracie's legs (2). Once Gracie is on the ground (3), he can maneuver into position for a triangle choke (4-5).

tion to deliver knee thrusts to their opponent. Perhaps the most devastating application of this technique occurred when Severn fought Oleg Taktarov in UFC V. After getting to the side mount on his sambo opponent, Severn inflicted several devastating knee smashes that split Taktarov's head open and stopped the fight.

Concluding Remarks

The mixed martial arts shine a light on the advantages and disadvantages of wrestling. Through MMA events, wrestlers have demonstrated the effectiveness of their techniques and conditioning and proved that their art provides a good base for that type of competition. But as practitioners of other styles adapt and weight classes are established, those skills alone are no longer sufficient.

None of this means that basic wrestling skills no longer have value in the mixed martial arts; rather, they should be applied selectively and with caution. At the same time, wrestlers should use the aforementioned tips to improve their performance—and their chances of finishing a match efficiently.

When Wrestlers Ruled the World

• Dan Severn, a Greco-Roman specialist with more than 70 titles, captured the championship at UFC V, the first Ultimate Ultimate, and the UFC IX superfight.

• Mark Coleman, a two-time All-American at Ohio State, a double gold medalist at the Pan American Games and a member of the 1992 U.S. Olympic team, was the UFC X and XI tournament champion and the UFC XII heavyweight victor.

• Randy Couture, the 1990, 1993 and 1997 U.S. Greco-Roman champion, was the UFC XIII heavyweight tournament champ, the UFC XV superfight winner, and the UFC Japan heavyweight champion.

• Mark Kerr, the 1992 NCAA champion at 190 pounds and a 1994 World Cup winner, has claimed two UFC heavyweight tournament victories at UFC XIV and UFC XV, as well as an eight-man tournament victory in Brazil.

• Kevin Jackson, an Iowa State wrestler and gold medalist at the 1992 Olympics, claimed the middleweight tournament championship at UFC XIV.

RICKSON
The Legend of No-Holds-Barred Fighting
Speaks Out on the State of the Grappling Arts
PART 1

Interview by Robert W. Young • March 2001

In the world of grappling and no-holds-barred competition, fighters come and go. Olympic wrestlers claw their way to the top, then sink to the bottom two months later when a good kick lays them out cold. Tough young Brazilians work their way up the ladder, then lose horribly to a street fighter with a strong overhand right. Yet one personality always seems to stay afloat. Rickson Gracie has taken on the best opponents the sport has to offer, and he has yet to lose a single match. But in the past few years, the 40-something fighting phenom has slowed his pace. Black Belt caught up with Gracie in Pacific Palisades, California, in search of answers to all those burning questions readers have been asking for months.

Black Belt: First, the big question: Are you retired?

Rickson Gracie: No.

BB: Do you have any fights planned?

Gracie: I haven't signed for any new fights, but there are always proposals I have to evaluate to see what's best for me. But I plan to fight only once a year, so I have time to decide when my next fight will be. In 2001, I will probably fight again.

BB: Will that be in the Colosseum, the Japanese event you competed in on May 26, 2000?

Gracie: The Colosseum was a great experience for me, but because I don't have a signed contract or an exclusive agreement with them, it is not certain. It's very possible but not for sure.

BB: What conditions do you think about when you're considering an offer to fight? The money? The location? The opponent?

Gracie: Of course, money, location and opponent, as well as the size of the event. But mainly what I look for is an event that will show the sport as a beneficial and positive influence for others. I am concerned about how the event will present itself, the goal behind the fight and the values of the organizers. I believe the Zen aspect of the martial arts is very important—including respect among fighters and the way an event is run.

BB: You want to be involved only with people who promote no-holds-barred fighting in a positive way, not in a violent way?

Gracie: Exactly.

BB: Some Brazilians recently told us that violence is a big part of the *jujutsu* scene in Brazil. They said the art's status used to be very high there, but now people think it is just a tool of street thugs. Is that true?

Gracie: Jujutsu is the fastest-growing sport in Brazil because everybody wants to be a fighter. Many students now think they have to fight to prove themselves. They train at a jujutsu school and go out to nightclubs to fight. For the past three or four years, that's been a big problem for Brazilian society. It's because a lot of gang members, tough guys and problem kids have jujutsu techniques put into their hands, and they become like little supermen. They beat everybody, and they create a lot of problems. This is the negative side, the wrong use of the power of jujutsu. Now in Brazil,

Instead of trying to execute his favorite technique in a match, Rickson Gracie (right) prefers to exploit whatever openings his opponent gives him.

people say, "Oh, anyone who trains in jujutsu normally creates problems." But that's not exactly what happens. Professionals who are involved in jujutsu try to develop the positive side of the art. Only the people who study jujutsu to cause trouble on the street bring this kind of bad image. But the police understand it's not a jujutsu thing; it's a criminal thing. It's the same as the way a lot of people use guns to commit crimes. Jujutsu training gives a sense of power, and people sometimes use it the wrong way.

BB: Have you noticed similar problems in the United States?

Gracie: No, because it's much harder here to solve disagreements by fighting. You can get sued, and the criminal justice system is much more effective here. In the United States, if you make a problem, you definitely will pay for it.

BB: Is it true that there's a rivalry in Brazil between jujutsu and *luta livre?*

Gracie: Yes and no. Yes because you can say there's even a kind of rivalry between jujutsu and jujutsu. We all compete with each other, but because we are practitioners of the same sport, this rivalry only goes to one level. Jujutsu people don't have that kind of thought for luta livre people. They don't think, "I'd like to beat him, but he is a nice guy because he practices the same sport as I do." Because it is only a similar sport, there is competition between jujutsu and luta livre practitioners. But things used to be much worse than they are. Now it's more respectful, and the students are starting to compete together in important international events. Things will get better until the problem disappears.

BB: Apparently not all jujutsu fighters in Brazil think so highly of other jujutsu fighters. For example, it seems like everyone in the Gracie family and a lot of people outside the family have a problem with Wallid Ismail, the man who choked out Royce on December 17, 1998. Why is that?

Gracie: Wallid is a very interesting character because he combines some special elements. He was never a great fighter, but he knows how to promote himself so that every time he has the opportunity, he makes it seem like he's always been the best and always will be the best. He says he can beat anyone easily and that he's done this and that. Everyone who has a normal sense of what is right and wrong thinks he goes a little overboard. But I don't have any hard feelings about Wallid because he's just ... never played in my league. I've never felt like he's someone I have to respect as a fighter. He's always been average.

BB: Do you think he's better at jujutsu than at NHB?

Gracie: Because he plays using endurance, using tactics to stall the fight—maybe with a *gi* he can get better results. In NHB, you have to be a more technical fighter, so he has more problems. I think he should stay in jujutsu.

BB: Why do you think Kazushi Sakuraba is so successful against Brazilian-jujutsu stylists?

Gracie: He doesn't make many mistakes. He's very calm. He's the kind of fighter who waits for you to make a mistake and then capitalizes on it. I saw fights where people kept pressure on him, like when he fought Kimo [Leopoldo], and he got beat up pretty easily. I saw fights where he didn't really win—like with Royler. Sakuraba stayed outside and kicked Royler's legs and punished him, and because of the weight difference, he got the advantage. I saw him fight Royce, and Royce had the advantage in the first rounds. And then he just got tired and could not keep the pressure

No-holds-barred fighting, in which the competitors do not wear a uniform, requires more technique than does ordinary grappling with a gi, says Gracie.

on Sakuraba. He could not finish the fight before he got tired. And I saw him fight Renzo. He was always very calm, waiting for Renzo to give him the space to create new options for himself. Basically, Sakuraba's not a destroyer; he's not a guy who has a great expertise in anything. But he's very smart and very tough. He's not afraid of getting beat up, and he plays with the crowd and makes a mess in his opponent's head.

BB: How does a person acquire that kind of mind-set? Could a fighter consciously develop his mind to use those same tricks against Sakuraba?

Gracie: I think you can develop that kind of mind, but some people are born with it. It's just that in every match Sakuraba has won, it was not a victory he could put over his shoulders [to display]. Of course, he deserved to win—he's a tough opponent. But he never made the victory. A lot of people allowed him to slip through their fingers. Nobody who lost to him says, "That guy is really good, he kicked my butt."

BB: So you don't see much technique in Sakuraba's fights?

Gracie: Of course he has technique, but I don't see anything that impresses me. The mental aspect of his game is the most valuable possession he has.

BB: Do you feel any pressure to fight Sakuraba—to protect the Gracie name, if for no other reason?

Gracie: I don't feel pressure to fight anybody because I don't have a commitment to myself to prove anything or to my family to protect the name. The family will always be respected. I don't think winning one more time or losing one more time will shake it. But in my heart, I really think Sakuraba deserves to get beat because it's like he's lucky all the time. He's just very slippery.

BB: If you don't fight him, who would have the best chance of beating him?

Gracie: A simple fighter can beat Sakuraba if he gets the enlightenment he needs to get the mental and psychological elements to guide him through the fight. Sakuraba is not a great puncher or a great submission fighter. He just stays calm and takes advantage of the openings. And if another fighter is calm enough to wait for his shot and tight enough to not give spaces and lose the opportunity, he can win.

BB: Frank Shamrock is confident that he can win.

Gracie: I believe so, too. But that doesn't mean that he cannot lose. Shamrock has, of course, the potential to beat Sakuraba. It's a matter of getting the strategic enlightenment.

BB: Could you say a little bit about your May 26, 2000, fight with

To improve your ability to move on the ground, Gracie recommends the following drill: Lie on your back with your partner in your guard (1). The partner stands up while holding your lapels and maintaining a good posture (2-3). You then lower your upper body toward the mat (4) and sit up (5). After a suitable number of repetitions, you reverse roles.

Masakatsu Funaki?

Gracie: He's famous in Japan. He played the highest game in his life, and afterward he retired. I have a lot of respect for all my opponents, but especially for him. He gave me his best. He tried to bring the fight, strategically speaking, to his strong element. He didn't want to give me opportunities—he's very knowledgeable about the way to do that—and he stuck with his plan. Things went my way when I created a little confusion, and then he lost his understanding of how things were going. After that, I kept the pressure on without giving him a chance to recover. I managed to win 11 minutes into the first round.

BB: Which technique did you use?

Gracie: Rear choke. Because the referee could not stop the fight—only the coach could throw in the towel or the fighter could tap out—once I squeezed him, the referee looked at me, and I felt like I had to let go because I didn't want to kill him. When I let go, he was already out. Nobody did anything, but I had this calm sense of what to do. If I had been emotionally involved, I could've kept squeezing forever.

BB: Was he a worthy opponent?

Gracie: Yes. Funaki is a strong guy. It was a tough fight. He prepared himself very hard. Things went my way, and I am happy about that. The only thing is, after that, he mentioned he was retiring. Of course, I respect his decision, but that's not my way of seeing things. I don't like to choose the backdoor when things get tough. Sometimes by losing we can be motivated to keep going.

RICKSON
The Legend of No-Holds-Barred Fighting Speaks Out on the State of the Grappling Arts
PART 2

Interview by Robert W. Young • April 2001

Black Belt: What is your current training routine?

Rickson Gracie: I have two ways to train: One is when I'm just teaching and trying to maintain my level. The other way is when I'm preparing for a fight. That's when I increase the intensity and the rest periods so I can recover and reach maximum performance.

BB: When you're not training for a fight, what does a typical day consist of?

Gracie: It always has some kind of recreational activity—like surfing, bike riding or some kind of cardio. And then I teach and eventually spar.

BB: Do you consider teaching a workout?

Gracie: Yes. It's not a very stressful workout or something I need to recover from, but I always break a sweat and get my blood circulating. I definitely get something from it.

BB: Do you lift weights?

Gracie: Sometimes prior to a fight, I exercise with weights.

BB: Is most of your sparring grappling, or do you also practice stand-up?

Gracie: I do a little bit of everything. But I always try to establish a purpose for my secondary training: to bring something to my abilities. I don't try to be the best in every segment of the martial arts.

BB: In a previous interview, you said you have no favorite technique—that you use whatever opening your opponent gives you. Is that still true?

Gracie: Definitely.

BB: Do you have a favorite way of ending a fight?

Gracie: As quickly as possible (laughs).

BB: Your fans might not like that because they won't get a chance to see a demonstration of Brazilian-*jujutsu* techniques.

Gracie: Yeah, that's a problem.

BB: What effect has your family had on the status of Brazilian jujutsu around the world?

Gracie: There has been an explosion of jujutsu. The exposure it has today is 100 times more than it had eight or 10 years ago. That has a lot of positive elements because Brazilian jujutsu has such a good reputation and good credibility. But there are also negative elements, such as when people think only of the effectiveness of jujutsu so they can display their power and superiority. They don't know that being a true warrior means you don't need to beat people or prove you're better. Because of them, some people think Brazilian-jujutsu fighters are like animals who don't

Although he does a little bit of everything in training, Gracie says he does not try to be the best at every form of fighting. His specialty is and always will be jujutsu.

understand the true martial arts. Personally, I am very concerned with balancing those two elements: the Zen aspect of the martial arts and the effectiveness of jujutsu.

BB: A few years ago, everyone thought Brazilian jujutsu was unbeatable. But now some people are defeating the best Brazilian fighters. Has that affected the state of the art?

Gracie: Always it is the individual that wins or loses. A fight is not won because of a technique or specific drill. It is won because of the physical, strategic, emotional and technical qualities of the fighter. At one point, Brazilian jujutsu was so unpredictable for other fighters that it was easy to win because no one knew what to expect. Now everyone knows. Now everyone trains in Brazilian jujutsu—even if they are boxers or karate experts or wrestlers. They develop a sense of where the danger is, and that brings the fight to a higher level. Fighters who practice Brazilian jujutsu now have to develop their other senses: their strategic sense, their heart, their emotional control. Sometimes those elements—if they have been

Instead of maneuvering into position to execute his favorite technique, Gracie prefers to react to the openings his opponent leaves.

developed so much during a fighter's life—will allow even a guy who has not trained a lot in Brazilian jujutsu to succeed without being technically superior. Now that the raw techniques of Brazilian jujutsu are not a secret anymore, you have to prove yourself as a fighter in a more general way.

BB: If a big wrestler on steroids acquires a basic understanding of jujutsu—enough to avoid leaving his arm to be trapped in an armbar, for example—is that a great advantage for him?

Gracie: Just being big and well-prepared is already a great advantage for him. That makes the smaller guy the underdog no matter what he does. I still believe it's possible for the smaller guy to win because a fight is not decided by the prevention of one technique. He has to create a nightmare, create smoke, then all the elements must be pushed to the limits. Even if he gets tired and confused, he has to be able to make quick decisions because that's when the opportunities start to pop up. It's hard to win quickly against a tough opponent.

BB: Do you think all NHB fighters—even those who deny it—train in jujutsu?

Gracie: They definitely have a sense of the positions they need to avoid and to develop that physical sense they have to practice.

BB: NHB competition was recently legalized in New Jersey and California. What effect will that have on the fledgling sport?

Gracie: As I follow the progress of NHB fighting, I try to stay balanced. I can't say it's great because a lot of people are still interested in wiping NHB from the face of the earth. For any promoter or producer to grow strong in the United States, he must have a plan for making a positive image for the sport. But once that is established, NHB can become bigger than boxing. If a positive image is not established, NHB will be only a fire in a light wood—a couple events will take place, but then someone with an ax will come and just cut it down. And we'll disappear.

BB: If an NHB show is presented in a positive way, do you think the sport will be able to get back on pay-per-view?

Gracie: I'm 100 percent sure that will be possible.

BB: Are you training any fighters who will be able to compete and help you promote those values?

Gracie: No professionals at this time.

BB: Why not?

Gracie: I cannot train a professional fighter if I'm still in the race. Soon I'll retire, and then I'll prepare my horses to win.

BB: How do you plan on contributing to the rise of the sport after you retire? Will you start an event of your own?

Gracie: Anything is possible. Right now, I don't think about the day after tomorrow; I'm too busy thinking about today, about the projects I have going on now. But I do plan to be involved not just in Brazilian jujutsu, but also in the positive development of the martial arts. That's my mission in life—to give people a sense of how the warrior spirit can make them more peaceful.

BB: Why aren't there any Rickson Gracie instructional videotapes on the market?

Gracie: Because I'm a perfectionist. I like to do my best. And I don't feel comfortable doing my best in a video and giving any guy with no respect for me, my family or my art a chance to pay $50 or $100 to buy everything I value. I prefer to teach people I trust—or at least people whose eyes I can look into. I have no interest in just becoming richer by selling tapes.

BB: You're saying that you don't want people you don't know to learn

Gracie's (left) mission in life is to teach people how the warrior spirit acquired through martial arts training can make their life more peaceful.

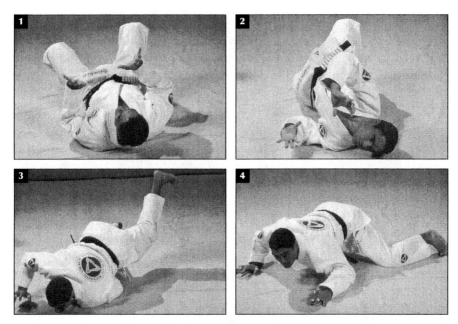

Positioning drill for ground speed and mobility: Gracie starts on his back (1). He turns his body to the left (2) and winds up on his stomach (3). He finishes on his hands and knees (4).

your techniques?

Gracie: It's not about "people I don't know," because I teach and I have in my association a lot of people I don't know. It's just about putting my heart and my essence up for sale without any interest in who's buying it or what benefit it's going to bring.

BB: Some martial artists believe that videotape cannot convey the highest teachings of any art. Do you regard "creating confusion"—the term you just mentioned—as the highest level of jujutsu?

Gracie: I think that's the highest level of any sport where you compete against a human being. It's different from surfing or skiing because in those sports you play against nature. When you have to create confusion, you have to flow in harmony. When you play against an opponent, you have to play all the different levels: mental, technical, concentration, intimidation, emotional and so on. Competition is very tricky because you are either the hunter or the prey. The confusion comes when things get involved—like you have to perform under pressure and you do it once, twice, three times as the pressure and confusion build. The decisions must be quicker, and even though you're prepared to do it, all those elements make you make mistakes. That's the sublime element that makes the difference between the champions and everybody else. It's how Michael Jordan performs when the pressure is on. I feel the same way in a fight. When things are boiling, I'm happy to be there. Every opponent is tough, but when things get messed up and you have to recover and do what you have to do in a fraction of a second, it can be challenging. Sometimes you do it one second late, and then for the next step, you do it two seconds late, and then it gets bigger and bigger and worse and worse.

BB: Ten years ago, there was no career path for NHB fighters in the United States who had reached such an advanced level. But now, mostly through the efforts of your family, practitioners have the option of becoming professional athletes. How does it feel to be responsible for a giant leap like that?

Gracie: I feel very good about it because once more of the population sees the benefits of jujutsu, the Gracie family will always have the option of continuing to do what it does. But it also brings more respect to society and enhances the whole element of being a professional in what I do. I'm proud to be part of that.

VITOR BELFORT
'The Phenom' of No-Holds-Barred Fighting Speaks Out!

by Robert W. Young • September 2001

When Vitor Belfort burst onto the American no-holds-barred scene in 1997, he was a young pup of 19. Although his lack of experience did not hamper his rapid rise to the top, it may have contributed to his fall. But he paid his dues in the following years and now seems to be on the road to recovery in NHB fighting and boxing. In the following Black Belt exclusive, the native of Rio de Janeiro talks about his checkered past and promising future.

—Editor

Black Belt: When you debuted in the Ultimate Fighting Championship XII at age 19, you were one of the most complete fighters ever to step into the octagon. How did you learn so much so soon?

Vitor Belfort: I did judo, wrestling and *jujutsu* when I was young, and I started boxing when I was 12. I fell in love with boxing and jujutsu, and I think I was the first fighter that mixed hand and ground techniques. That's why I was successful.

BB: Is it true that you could've gone to the Olympics as a boxer?

Belfort: I tried, but I got hurt before the trials, and the date of the trials cannot be changed because it's the Olympics. I missed my chance, but I'm not going to wait for the next Olympics; I'm going to start pro boxing.

BB: If that career path takes off, will you quit NHB fighting?

Belfort: I'm very sad because I was the youngest fighter ever to win the UFC, and the fans appreciated what I did. But the politicians didn't like the sport and there were no sponsors, so it never became really popular in America. Because I'm only 24, I still have a chance to explode in the sport. But if boxing opens the door for me, I cannot just close it. I'd rather be getting paid in my sport, however.

BB: What's the hardest part about boxing? Do you have to change the way you fight?

Belfort: In boxing, you've got to relax more. You've got to stay on your feet and move around. You've got to have combinations and defense all the time. That's different from NHB fighting, which can go on and off during a match. In boxing, you don't need to worry that somebody's going to attack your legs or kick you, so boxing is much easier—but at the same time, it's harder because you've got to throw combinations, counter and move.

BB: Do you think boxing and jujutsu are the perfect combination for NHB fighting?

Belfort: The perfect combination is to know boxing, jujutsu, wrestling, kicking and how to make your body fast. If you have a good ability in all aspects of fighting, you can be a complete fighter.

BB: It was reported that you recently suffered an injury.

Belfort: Yes. When I fought [Kazushi] Sakuraba in PRIDE 5 in April 1999, a lot of people said, "Vitor sold himself to Sakuraba." But I've never done that in my life. I don't want to take anything away from Sakuraba because he proved he's a very good fighter—one of the best in the world—but two weeks before the match, I had knee surgery. And when I got to Japan and weighed in, they made me lose 20 pounds. But I always try to be professional, and I didn't want to disappoint my fans and the promoters. I tried to rehabilitate my knee, but I didn't have time to get in shape. But

 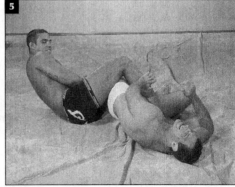

Vitor Belfort stands near his opponent and holds his left heel (1). He shifts the heel to his other hand (2), then drops to deliver a punch to the chin (3). Next, Belfort wraps his left arm around the opponent's trapped leg (4) and falls backward to secure an ankle lock (5).

I had to step in the ring. In the first four minutes, my knee went out. I put it back in place and fought another 15 minutes. I knew I couldn't do it, but I said to myself, "I've got to stay here until the last minute and try to do something."

But then I broke my hand. Sakuraba saw something was wrong with me, and he wasn't looking for a grappling fight. He was just scoring points by kicking and doing stuff like that. I tried to take the fight to the ground because I couldn't punch with all the pain. But he didn't want to grapple with me because he was winning and didn't want to risk anything. In his other matches, he took risks, but not with me. He ended up winning. But I want a rematch—and I would like to get it in the States.

BB: Is there any way to predict how you could beat him?

Belfort: You never know what's going to happen. The fight changes from one minute to the next. You've got to be focused and ready for anything.

BB: Do you see any weaknesses in his game?

Belfort: He is very predictable. Everybody knows what he does. But I think the best weapon Sakuraba has is that he's coldblooded. He feels fear, but he doesn't show it. He knows how to control his emotions.

BB: And if you know that about him, it helps you?

Belfort: Of course.

BB: It seems like many Brazilian grapplers have lost to Sakuraba. What's the attitude in Brazil about him? Is everyone there thinking, "How can I beat Sakuraba?"

Belfort: He has not beaten a lot of Brazilians. After he fought me, he got famous. Before that, he was nobody. After he fought me, people thought, "Oh, Vitor got paid to fight Sakuraba and lose. Now we're going to get less people to beat Japanese guys." And they thought he was easy. And then he went against Royler Gracie [in PRIDE 8]. I think Royler's a great fighter, but he's never really fought anyone. He's a lightweight. He thought, "I have the name, maybe I can win here," and he lost to Sakuraba.

BB: But Royler Gracie isn't the only Brazilian to lose to Sakuraba.

Belfort: And then they figured, "Royler lost to a heavyweight [because] he's very light. So they got Royce Gracie. Royce hadn't fought for four years. Then he stepped in the ring with Sakuraba [in the PRIDE Grand Prix 2000] and lost. And they figured, "OK, Royce lost. Who's next?"

It's not about who you are; it's about how you fight. In NHB fighting, it's not about jujutsu or your family name. It's about how you train, how good your cardio is, how you punch and kick, and if you have explosiveness and strength. Everything works together.

Belfort holds the opponent in his open guard (1). The opponent stands, and Belfort grabs his left knee as he spins his body counterclockwise (2). Once he is in position, Belfort positions his left leg over his opponent's head (3). He then forces him to the mat and locks his right arm (4). Note how Belfort's control of the opponent's left leg increases the security of the hold.

BB: Are you confident you could beat Sakuraba in a rematch?

Belfort: Sure. The problem is politics. In Japan, the people who control him don't want to let him fight me because they don't want to risk his fame. I don't blame Sakuraba for that.

BB: Is your hand completely recovered from the injury you sustained in PRIDE 5?

Belfort: I have no problems at all now. I have fought already. After [the first match with] Sakuraba, I had three fights: Gilbert Yvel in PRIDE 9, Daijiro Matsui in PRIDE 10 and Bob Southworth in PRIDE 13. My hands made them mad.

BB: Did you win all three matches?

Belfort: Yes. My record is now 16-2. Every time I fight now, I do something different because I want people to see what I can do. People used to say, "Vitor doesn't have cardio," or "Vitor can only fight for 10 minutes." But I've fought for 20 minutes, and I could fight for one hour. People are starting to realize that. I just want to make the fans happy and put on an exciting fight.

BB: People started questioning your endurance because in your early UFC bouts, you beat everybody in a couple minutes. You were at the top of the mountain, but then you went down when you had to endure longer matches.

Belfort: Not "went down." I just lost a few fights. That happens. But when you lose, some people want to bring you down. I hope the new UFC owners don't try to do that because everybody loses. You cannot judge a fighter from one fight; you judge him from his career.

BB: Some people have said that because you won so easily in the beginning, you became overconfident.

Belfort: Yeah. Because I was very young, I got a little cocky. I relaxed a little. I started thinking, "I did it before in five minutes, and I can do it again." But then I fought Sakuraba, a guy who was smart, talented, experienced and in great shape. I wasn't ready for that fight.

BB: Even so, a lot of people expected you to win.

Belfort: I bet if I fight him again, I can beat him.

BB: Do you have any idea when that might happen?

Belfort: I will take a rematch any time, but the fans have to want it and the money has to be there.

BB: Is there anyone that you would just like to fight for the challenge of it?

Belfort: Frank Shamrock would be a very good match. But they would have to pay him and me well. That's what I like: a challenge that pays well and that the fans want.

BB: Do you still compete as part of the Carlson Gracie team?

Belfort: No. I am now part of the Brazilian Top Team. Once I broke with Carlson, everybody broke with him. We made the Brazilian Top Team—me, Ricardo Liborio, Murilo Bustamante, Mario Sperry and all the old black belts from Carlson.

BB: At the beginning of your career, you fought as Vitor Gracie, not Vitor Belfort. Did your relationship with Carlson Gracie have anything to do with that?

Belfort: Carlson wanted to put that name on my belt. But my family didn't agree because we thought, "If I win, they're going to give all the recognition to the Gracie family." Using the name "Belfort" turned out to be a good idea for another reason: Now that the Gracies are not on top, people don't [associate] me with them.

BB: Some people have said that steroids played a part in your rise to the top.

Belfort: That's false. A lot of people say things. I just went off my diet and got a little fat. I didn't train; I was just lifting weights. I relaxed. And people talked. Everybody likes to put you down when you're somebody. There's a lot of jealousy in this business.

Belfort uses his arms and legs to control his opponent (1). He then employs his right leg to immobilize the other man's lead leg as he scoots forward and grabs his torso (2). Belfort leverages the opponent to the mat (3) and reaches under his right leg (4). To finish, he rotates around the opponent's leg as he shifts to the opposite side of his body, hyperextending his knee for the submission (5).

BB: You're now winning again. Do you attribute that to any new techniques or any old techniques that you've recently mastered?

Belfort: Everybody has favorite techniques, but they never say what they are.

BB: Do you try to get into positions where you can use your favorite techniques?

Belfort: Yes. But NHB is fun because you never know what's going to happen. You cannot depend on being able to use a favorite technique, because if somebody blocks you, it might not be an option.

BB: In the beginning, it seemed like the guard was the secret weapon of Brazilian fighters, but now many Japanese and American fighters know how to defeat it.

Belfort: NHB is not like it was. A lot of Japanese and American fighters have created new techniques. Everybody knows what everybody else is going to do. The most important thing in fighting is now your cardio—how long you can last and how much you can explode.

BB: What do you do for cardio?

Belfort: My trainer and I do things crazy—totally different from what everybody else does. The routine has running, fighting and weightlifting.

BB: What other attributes does a person need to succeed in NHB?

Belfort: Physical strength.

BB: What about the mind?

Belfort: You've got to have the mind, too. You've got to have everything. If I couldn't have everything, I would prefer to have the conditioning and the mind—and then comes the technique.

BB: What's the biggest mistake you see fighters making these days?

Belfort: Many of them don't train right because the money and the exposure are missing. If a fighter doesn't think, "I've got to train hard because my fans are watching me," he won't get better. Everybody's got to have something to motivate himself.

BB: In your opinion, who are the best fighters out there now?

Belfort: You have Sakuraba, Frank Shamrock, Mark Kerr, Mark Coleman, Igor Vovchanchyn—a bunch of good fighters.

BB: If the money is right, you're willing to fight any one of them?

Belfort: Yes. I fought a couple of them already.

BB: How will your next performance—whether it's against one of those fighters or someone else—compare with your early fights? Do you think it will be as impressive?

Belfort: Every time I fight, I want to impress. I give my best, impress

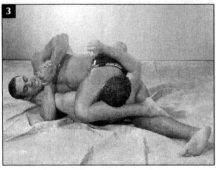

Belfort assumes the side-control position on his opponent (1). He grasps his opponent's right arm and forces it down until he can use his left thigh to restrain it (2). After Belfort strikes his opponent's face, he slides his left leg across his face and wraps it around his neck. At the same time, he locks the opponent's left arm (3).

the fans, make a good show, and the promoters like it. I want to give back what they pay me for. I want to give them two times more than what they give me.

BB: When you debuted in the UFC, you displayed some of the most impressive punching skills anyone had ever seen. Do you have any kind of tricks like that planned for the future?

Belfort: I have a lot of tricks planned. Just wait and see. I have settled down and started training. You are going to see a lot of excitement.

FIRE AND ICE
Four Surefire Grappling Techniques, Courtesy of Chuck 'The Iceman' Liddell
by Sara Fogan and Robert W. Young • October 2001

A new fighter has battled his way to the top of the middleweight food chain. He doesn't talk a lot of trash before his bouts, and he doesn't humiliate his opponents afterward. Face to face in street clothes, he is as personable as the guy next door. But as soon as he's unleashed in the octagon, the Jekyll-Hyde transformation commences. The quiet and unassuming martial artist morphs into a calm, cool assassin. He becomes Chuck "The Iceman" Liddell.

The versatile warrior has repeatedly proved that his stand-up skills are enough to efficiently eliminate virtually any opponent he faces in the ring. The San Luis Obispo, California, resident claims he built that portion of his NHB arsenal from a base of *koei-kan* karate, *kenpo*, kickboxing and boxing. The other half of his repertoire comes from *jujutsu* and wrestling, as well as a little homegrown submission wisdom from the school of hard knocks. It is the latter of "Liddell-*ryu*"—specifically two variations of two proven submission techniques—that this article will focus on.

Kneebar From the Top

The kneebar is an effective finishing technique that can be executed from the half-guard, whether you are on the top or bottom. The key is setting up your opponent and catching him by surprise.

If your opponent is lying on his back and you are held in his half-guard, straddling his right leg, you should redirect his attention toward his upper body by appearing to attack his arms. As soon as he is distracted, slip your outside (left) knee across his abdomen and lift his left knee. Next, continue your motion across his body and fall to his left side while using your arms to pin the leg against your chest. As you arch your back, your hips exert pressure against his knee and your right leg keeps him from maneuvering to relieve it.

"The main thing is to get his leg up as high as you can and sit back while holding it as tight as you can," says Liddell. "That makes the move really hard to get out of."

A common mistake martial artists make when they execute this version of the kneebar is being in a hurry and not keeping their hips tight against the opponent's thigh. If he can slide his knees out from between your legs after you cross his body and fall to the mat, you won't be able to maintain control of it or hyperextend the joint to finish him.

If the opponent blocks you or if you have trouble getting your leg all the way across his body, you can sit on his chest and then reverse the direction of your pull. That will mean you end up falling to his right side instead of his left, but you will have trapped the same leg using the same relative body positioning. The main difference is that you will use your left arm to hook behind his knee and your right to secure his heel.

Kneebar from the top: Tito Ortiz (bottom) holds Chuck Liddell in his half-guard (1). Liddell distracts his opponent by appearing to attack his arms, then sits up and places his left leg across his abdomen while lifting his left knee (2). Liddell falls to the opponent's left side (3a) and uses his arms and hips to apply pressure to the knee (4a). If the opponent interferes with the plan of attack, Liddell can use his left arm to control the leg (3b) and fall to the opponent's right side to execute the kneebar (4b).

Kneebar from the bottom: Liddell holds Ortiz in his half-guard (1). He places his right arm under Ortiz's right arm and his left arm behind Ortiz's right knee, with his left calf in the crook of his opponent's left leg (2). Using his right shin to lift, Liddell rotates Ortiz counterclockwise and hooks his left leg over his butt (3). Even as Ortiz twists to attempt an escape, Liddell maintains his hold on the leg and hyperextends the limb (4). Close-up of the final position (5).

Kneebar From the Bottom

When you are on your back with your opponent in your half-guard, your first priority is to break his balance and roll him to one side. As he kneels over you on your left side, turn so you are facing him. Slip your right arm under his armpit and your left arm behind his right knee. Press your left calf into the back of his left knee and your right shin into his stomach. Next, use your right arm to push him and your right leg to lift him as you rotate his body counterclockwise away from your head. Immediately hook your left leg over his butt while you pin his right knee against your chest, then execute the kneebar by arching your back to apply pressure against the joint.

"You have to keep your hips close to his and prevent his leg from twisting," says Liddell. "You want to try to keep his knee straight into your chest,

because if he turns his leg and sits up, it will take the pressure off his knee."
If the opponent is less than expert at escaping, however, you should be able
to roll with him and maintain your submission hold on his leg.

Heel Hook From the Bottom

It is possible to effect a heel hook when your opponent is mounted on
top of you, but first you must get out of the mount. Place your hands on
his lower abdominal area and your forearms on his thighs, then thrust
your hips upward and push his body to your right. At the same time, turn
toward him (to your right) and place your right leg between his legs as
you use your right arm to push his upper body away. Next, throw your left
leg across his right thigh and arch your back to get your butt as close as

Heel hook from the bottom: When Ortiz mounts
Liddell, Liddell immediately places his hands on
the opponent's abdomen and his forearms on his
thighs (1). Liddell then thrusts his hips upward and
pushes Ortiz to his right (2). Once the opponent is
dislodged, Liddell turns toward him and puts his
right leg between his legs (3). Liddell throws his
left leg across the opponent's right leg, positions
his hips close to the opponent's hips, and traps the
opponent's right foot under his left arm (4). To finish,
he wraps his left arm around the heel and applies
pressure (5).

possible to his while you trap his right foot under your left arm. To finish him, reach back with your left hand and scoop his trapped heel with your forearm. Lock your hands for added power and twist your torso clockwise to apply pressure to his heel.

The heel hook can pop an opponent's knee and ankle because both joints are twisted at the same time. Owing to its devastating nature, many fighters have learned to defend against it.

"If the opponent is good on the mount, it's hard to get that separation to get your leg in," says Liddell. A skilled fighter may also be able to escape by pointing his toes and rolling as he tries to pull his leg free. But once you start cranking the heel, it's hard for anyone to break out.

Heel Hook From the Half-Guard

You can also employ the heel hook while lying on your back, holding your opponent in your half-guard. Start by placing your right shin against

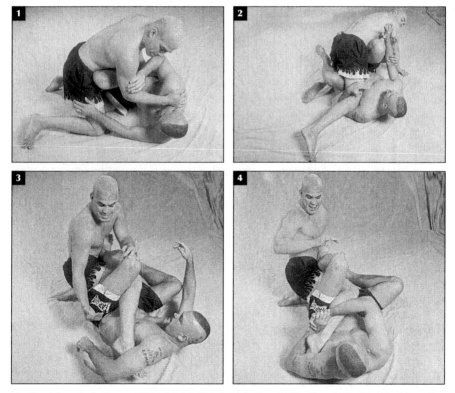

Heel hook from the half-guard: Liddell holds Ortiz in his half-guard (1). After placing his right shin against the opponent's stomach, Liddell uses his right arm and leg to shove Ortiz away (2). The positioning allows Liddell to place his left leg across the opponent's right thigh and trap his left foot under his arm (3). From there, the heel hook is executed by positioning his left forearm under the heel and exerting pressure toward the right (4).

his stomach and controlling his right leg with your left arm. Then use your right arm and leg to shove his upper body away from your head. If he cooperates, you can execute a kneebar from the bottom as described above. If he changes his direction and starts to sit back into you, you should hook his foot under your left armpit and use your forearm to apply lateral pressure to his heel.

Once he realizes what you are attempting, he probably will not be able to strike you because he will be working to keep you off his heel. "Even if he does try to punch, he won't be able to generate a lot of power because your left leg will be over his body and he can't throw a punch across your legs very easily," says Liddell.

A common error involves failing to place your leg over the opponent's leg or allowing him to extend his leg during the execution of the technique. To do the heel hook, you need his leg to be bent and under your leg.

Just Part of the Game

The kneebar and the heel-hook variations are great for catching an opponent, particularly one who isn't overly familiar with leg locks. They work even better if you distract him with punches to the head. Nevertheless, it is always possible that he will know how to counter the techniques and gain a superior position.

Liddell warns, "Any time you're being offensive—especially in submission fighting—you risk losing [your] position, but risk is part of the game. Maintaining an advantage in a fight is about being aware of your opponent's capabilities. It's knowing what someone else can do, what his counters will be, and if that happens, how to react so it doesn't cost you the fight."

ULTIMATE BATTLE PLAN
Four Tremendous Takedowns From UFC Bad-Boy Tito Ortiz

by Sara Fogan • December 2001

Looks can be deceiving. Take Ultimate Fighting Championship light-heavyweight Tito Ortiz. When he steps into the octagon and the door is locked behind him, he is pure attitude and devastation. But when he is away from the bright lights and fanfare, he could almost be the guy next door. Charming, friendly and polite, the Huntington Beach, California, resident is a far cry from the "Bad Boy" persona he projects before a fight.

Perhaps the truest assessment of the real Tito Ortiz is that he's a serious athlete who constantly strives to improve his game. Like other top no-holds-barred fighters, he values cross-training and learning skills from other martial artists, and he counts UFC 31 heavyweight champion Chuck Liddell, *Black Belt* Hall of Fame member Blinky Rodriguez, and John Lewis—a Gene LeBell black belt—as his regular training partners. Ortiz trains for eight hours a day, seven days a week, and follows a strict regimen that includes *muay Thai* kickboxing, *jujutsu*, cardio workouts, running and weightlifting. In addition, he rolls with the entire Golden West Junior College wrestling team several times a week.

Although he has been competing in NHB events for only four years, Ortiz has used his finely honed skills to leave an indelible impression on fans and pundits alike. Sporting blond hair and a pair of training shorts bursting with orange flames, the 6-foot-2-inch, 225-pound fighter is a

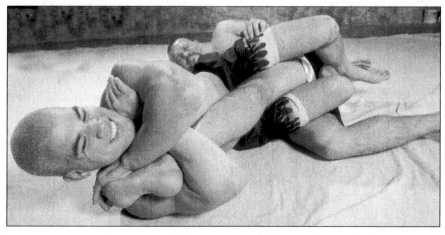

A good takedown can open the door for any type of submission technique, says Tito Ortiz (left, with Chuck Liddell).

warrior who takes no prisoners when he goes for the final clinch. With a 7-2-0 UFC record, he has no qualms about using any of the techniques in his arsenal to submit his opponents. The following are four of those techniques—Ortiz's favorite takedowns. Master them and you'll be one step closer to fighting like the champ.

Double-Leg Takedown

The double-leg takedown is good to use when someone comes at you with his fists flying, Ortiz says. The first thing you should do is upset his balance, and to accomplish this, you must squat down as you close the

Double-leg takedown: Ortiz and Liddell square off. Ortiz squats to change his level, then explodes forward to close the gap (2). He uses his head to push against the opponent's chest, keeping him off-balance, and his arms to control the opponent's thighs, preventing him from sprawling (3). Ortiz steps forward, lifts the opponent and slams him to the mat (4). He finishes by placing his left knee on his opponent's stomach to maintain control as he executes a finishing technique (5).

gap. Next, step forward, place your head against the middle of his chest and lift him off his feet until his body is horizontal, he says.

It is important to get your hips under your adversary's and control his thighs with your hands so he can't sprawl, Ortiz adds. Once he hits the mat, put your knee on his stomach and execute your preferred finishing or knockout technique.

The biggest mistake fighters make when trying to execute the double-leg takedown in the ring is being overconfident, Ortiz says. The best way to overcome that obstacle is to train diligently. "If you want to learn a move like the double-leg, do it as many times as you can until you get it stuck in your head," he says. "Repetition is a huge thing for mastering a takedown."

Underhook Single-Leg Takedown

The underhook single-leg takedown is another effective technique to use when you are facing a Thai boxer or a striker who likes to tie up his opponent, Ortiz says. Start by using your left arm to underhook your adversary's right arm and close the gap between you. Your right arm allows you to control the distance between your torso and his. Next, drop your right arm and wrap it around his lower right thigh while you maintain contact with his right arm or shoulder, he says. "This gets him off-balance and you into position for the single-leg takedown."

Alternatively, you can press your head against his chest to gain leverage and keep him off-balance, he adds.

Once you have him in position for the takedown, step forward with your right leg, switching the position of your feet so your left is now in front. Next, lock your hands behind his knee and slide your grip down his leg. To force him to the ground, use your upper body to drive him backward while you hug his trapped leg. Once he's down, put your knee on his stomach to hold him in position while you finish him, Ortiz says.

It is imperative to keep your head on the inside of your opponent's body once you trap and lift his leg, Ortiz warns. Unskilled fighters often allow their head to slip to the outside, and that can expose them to a guillotine choke. "And if you're facing the outside, it just gets into a scramble and the takedown can be a lot harder to do," he adds.

Body-Lock Slam

In addition to being an effective takedown strategy, the body-lock slam can knock the wind out of your opponent, momentarily stunning him,

Underhook single-leg takedown: As he ties up with Liddell, Ortiz uses his left arm to underhook the opponent's right arm (1). He then reaches down to grab the opponent's right leg (2). After locking his hands around the leg, Ortiz lifts it (3) and leverages the opponent to the ground (4). Once he lands, Ortiz places his right knee on the opponent's stomach to control him while he strikes (5).

Ortiz says. To execute the technique, you must start from an underhook position in which your left arm is wrapped around your adversary's right shoulder. Your left foot should be even with his right when you extend your right arm under his left arm to set up the body lock, he says. Next, step forward with your right leg to get your hips under his hips. Clasp your hands in a Greco-style lock at the center of his back, bend your knees and lift him off the ground before you turn his body, slam him to the mat and finish him, Ortiz says.

When he is off the ground, he will be unable to move his hips away from you to sprawl, the UFC champ says. That makes escape virtually impossible.

Speed and 100-percent commitment are the most important components of an effective body-lock slam, Ortiz says. If you do not move quickly enough, your adversary could tumble away from you or try to get a body lock on you, he warns.

Cobra Choke

The cobra choke serves as a takedown method and a submission technique, Ortiz says. To effect it, use your left arm to reach under your opponent's right arm until you get the underhook position. Next, pull his head down with your right arm, wrap that arm around his neck and hook

Body-lock slam: As Ortiz and Liddell clinch, Ortiz underhooks his opponent's right arm (1). He then shifts his weight forward and wraps his right arm around the other man's torso, clasping his hands in a Greco-style lock behind his back (2). Next, Ortiz maneuvers his hips under his opponent's hips and lifts him (3). After dropping the other fighter on the mat (4), Ortiz controls him with his knee and prepares to punch (5).

Cobra choke: Ortiz faces his opponent (1). As the opponent moves in to strike, Ortiz uses his left arm for an underhook and his right to control the head (2). He then uses his left arm to reach across the opponent's back and grab his latissimus muscle while wrapping his right arm around his neck (3). Ortiz steps forward, twists the other man to the mat and forces his chin toward his stomach for the submission (4).

his chin with your hand; that will enable you to control his head and achieve a dominant position, he says.

Once you've taken control of his head, reach your left arm across your adversary's back and grab his left latissimus muscle, Ortiz says. Maintain your hold on his chin at all times and keep his head pinned in your armpit. Next, step forward with your right foot and twist his torso until he falls onto his left side. Once he's on the ground, keep his chin tight against your right hip and pull his head toward his stomach until he submits.

A savvy opponent may be able to peel your hand off his chin and move his right arm over your head to create a gap through which he can escape, Ortiz warns. If that happens, you can simply change tactics and go for a leg hook, side mount or full mount to regain the advantage, he says. The key to being able to transition into a different attack—during this or any of the other three takedowns—lies in having practiced the moves over and over in the *dojo*.

WILL THE REAL BAS RUTTEN PLEASE STAND?

by Stephen Quadros • Photo by Robert W. Young • Grappling & NHB 2001

Thailand is revered as the Mecca of all things muay Thai. But because the majority of Thailand's greatest champions are in the lower weight divisions, Holland has garnered a growing legacy as the most formidable producer of stand-up heavyweight fighters. The Dutch are also developing a proud heritage in the free-fight game, also known as no-holds-barred or mixed martial arts. What a Dutch freestyle fighter lacks in ground and submission skills, he will make up with an outrageous capacity for striking devastation.

One of the godfathers of NHB fighting in Holland is Bas Rutten. Originally a taekwondo and kyokushin-kai karate stylist, he climbed to the No. 2 spot in his weight division in kickboxing while training at the Maeng-Ho gym. Then he was invited to participate in Japan's Pancrase Hybrid Wrestling in 1991.

After losing to a few of the best grappling-oriented fighters, Rutten made up his mind to learn the ground game. The result was a feat that no one has since duplicated: Rutten moved to the United States and, after two fights, became the UFC heavyweight champion.

—S.Q.

Black Belt: These days, you seem to be busy in the film and TV business. What's going on?

Bas Rutten: I've got some movies coming out. I just guest-starred in an episode of *Freedom.* Joel Silver *(Lethal Weapon, The Matrix)* produces it. It's a great show about the not-too-distant future. The economy has collapsed, and the military government has taken over. The good people are the resistance fighters. In episode No. 6, they bring me in as Capt. Stark, an anti-terrorist guy. I am informed that the resistance fighters are terrorists. I am pretty violent. It will be a recurring role. But we don't know yet if the series will get picked up. I was originally hired to train the lead actor to have a special military-type fighting style. Once I was there, I started doing all the fight choreography. Then they saw my tape and gave me an acting part. Also, I will go to Italy soon for a movie called *Ancient Warriors.* It stars Gary Busey and Jim Belushi. In January, I will probably be working on another movie.

BB: What does all the film work do to your fighting career?

Rutten: It puts it in second place.

BB: There are rumors of your retirement.

Rutten: Right now, it looks like I'm retired. I'm still hurt. I still have therapy for my shoulder. My knee is not 100 percent, and my left arm is

After an amazingly quick rise to the top of the
NHB ladder, Bas Rutten (top) has decided to
retire to pursue acting.

not good—all these little things—so for the moment, I am retired because I have a lot of offers. If I do something, I do it 100 percent. If I do acting, it will be with that kind of commitment. I really don't have enough time to train properly for fighting.

BB: How do you like being an NHB commentator?

Rutten: I love it—especially when I've worked with you [during numerous PRIDE shows]. You are a very good professional commentator. I did a little fill-in here and there.

BB: It's always a pleasure working with you because you are so funny. And you obviously have a great deal of hands-on knowledge and the gift of gab. Does commentating make you nervous?

Rutten: Yes, everything makes you nervous the first time. The good thing is that I did it with you. Because you're very accomplished, you kept everything going when I screwed up.

BB: Do you think that commentating has a parallel psychologically to fighting—with respect to dealing with pressure and thinking on your feet?

Rutten: For sure. Because I used to fight, I know what's going through their mind. I like to call things before they happen—like when a guy is on top and I say, "He should do this and that." And finally he does it. It's fun when you can call it before it happens. It's also good to *not* be in the ring and still be there [at ringside].

BB: Is there anything else you would like to add?

Rutten: The only thing I want to say is that last week I saw for the first time the fight between Jose "Pele" Landi-Jons and Jorge "Macaco" Patino. (laughs) It's their first fight.

BB: There is an obvious rivalry between the two men, and the fight has some rather unorthodox moves by Pele.

Rutten: It is one of the best fights I've ever seen. To the readers of *Black Belt:* If you haven't seen it, find a tape because it's unbelievable.

FRANK SHAMROCK SHINES IN THE RING AND ON CAMERA

by Ella Morse • Photo by Todd Felderstein • Grappling & NHB 2001

In November 1999, Ultimate Fighting Championship middleweight titleholder Frank Shamrock fought—and was soundly defeated by—an unlikely opponent: former karate champion Chuck Norris.

Sound incredible? Well, it happened—sort of. The fight actually was a scene in a *Walker, Texas Ranger* episode, and Shamrock's turn at acting proved he's got as much talent in front of the camera as he has in the octagon.

"Everyone [on the set] was concerned that I wouldn't know how to stop or that I wouldn't know how to *not* be a fighter," Shamrock said of filming the fight scenes.

Needless to say, his performance on the hit series impressed viewers as well as the cast and crew. He learned his lines and pulled his punches, and no one ended up seeing stars the way Igor Zinoviev did when he faced the champ in UFC XVI.

Shamrock has been a professional NHB fighter since 1994. His adopted brother, Ken Shamrock, introduced him to submission fighting when he was 22. Frank joined hi brother's professior

In match after match, Frank Shamrock (left) has proved that he is one of the most versatile and accomplished martial artists in NHB fighting.

fighting team, the Lion's Den, on April 4, 1994, and defeated Bas Rutten to win the Pancrase title in Japan on December 16 of that year.

Frank left the Lion's Den in 1997, but his success in the ring has continued. He went on to defeat other great fighters, such as Enson Inoue and Tito Ortiz. and it took him a mere 22 seconds to best Olympic gold-medal wrestler Kevin Jackson in the Ultimate Japan in 1997.

Shamrock trains with former UFC heavyweight champion and veteran kickboxer Maurice Smith, and he has also worked out with UFC XII middleweight tournament champion Jerry Bohlander and UFC XIII middleweight tournament champ Guy Mezger. Shamrock's success in the ring may be attributed to his varied martial arts skills: He is well versed in stand-up styles, such as boxing and kickboxing, as well as submission fighting and freestyle wrestling.

"I've been a champion of six different organizations, but it's not what I've won or what I've done that makes me a success," Shamrock said. "I've taken an influx of all these martial arts and combined them into one and tested them at the highest levels."

His hard work and focus also played a role in his rise to the top. He has often said that a talented fighter's desire to win in the ring ultimately determines whether he will achieve his goal. And he is living proof of that model. When he's preparing for a fight, he trains five hours a day, five days a week—including weights, cardio, boxing, kickboxing, submissions and takedowns. Before he steps into the ring, he meditates and does deep-breathing exercises to focus on how he will defeat his opponent.

Now limiting his fighting to once a year, Shamrock dismisses the idea of retiring from NHB to enter the world of professional wrestling. Instead, he wants to devote more time to teaching and training other fighters and furthering his acting career. The only fight that interests him is a match against Japanese wrestler and NHB sensation Kazushi Sakuraba. Although Sakuraba defeated Royce, Royler and Renzo Gracie in different PRIDE events, Shamrock is confident that he would beat the wrestler if they faced each other in the ring. He is currently negotiating to fight Sakuraba in a new NHB event called Strike Force.

Some pundits consider the 28-year-old Shamrock to be one of the greatest fighters of the past decade. That he will one day bow out of the fight circuit for good will likely disappoint his legions of fans. However, no one can deny that Shamrock has put in his dues and has had a tremendous run in the wild world of NHB fighting.

LEADER OF THE PACK
In the UFC's Lightweight Division, Pat Miletich Rules!

by Christa Light • Photos courtesy of dojotv.com • Grappling and NHB 2001

The overhead lights are bright. The roar of the crowd is deafening. The fans are cheering. But all the noise and confusion remain on the outside of the cage. On the inside, five-time UFC lightweight champ Pat Miletich is totally focused on the fight and barely aware of the din that surrounds him.

This story ends when the fight begins. It's not about Pat Miletich and his titles and accomplishments. It's about the Pat Miletich that we can't see when he steps into the cage. It's about what he does away from the crowd and the cameras that allows him to step into the cage as a formidable opponent and step out as a world champion.

Background

Miletich started wrestling during his elementary-school years in Iowa. While most of his early matches ended in his opponent's favor, he continued to train and wrestle until he was in college. He usually worked on a new technique for at least an hour, sometimes learning only two or three moves during a four-hour practice. But by the end of practice, he knew those moves. He attributes much of his fighting prowess today to the solid combination of that work ethic and the sense of balance and control he learned as a wrestler.

"I recognized the need to be well-rounded early on," he says. "I never considered myself a world-class athlete, so I knew that I had to outwork my opponent to win. One of the most important things I would tell any young wrestling hopeful is that you have to drill technique—drill, drill, drill. And when you get sick of drilling, drill some more. Drill until each move becomes an automatic response."

After leaving college, Miletich took up kickboxing to keep in shape. He then branched out into karate and Brazilian *jujutsu*. He enjoyed the challenge of stand-up fighting and went on to study *muay Thai*—and did so well that he became a Midwest champion. He also competed in several professional boxing matches. However, one point Miletich emphasizes is that he does not consider himself to be the best in any one of those martial arts. Rather, he is very good in all of them. And it's that multidimensional depth that has helped him become a UFC champion.

"I've learned what positions to stay out of—like you just don't stand in front of a good striker," he says. "But my first strategy is always to know my opponent. For example, is he better on his feet or on the ground? I want to lessen any chance he has to do damage. It's like a mental chess match. You learn the moves, focus on the game and then wait for your opponent to make a mistake."

This requires patience, which Miletich believes can be developed only through training and experience: "Patience must begin on your first day in the gym. You drill to perfect your technique, hour after hour with countless repetitions. Then you work up the levels one by one—more fights, better skills, better opponents—until you get to the top. And that's where it starts. The top is a beginning, not an end. It's where you've finally pulled it all together and can really start to make it work."

Miletich believes that all martial artists need to keep an open mind about modifying and combining styles to find the most effective combination for

Striking skills play an important role in the ring for Miletich. He wants his opponents to fear him on his feet as well as on the mat.

Muay Thai forms the foundation of Miletich's close-range striking techniques.

them. He also believes that many instructors will unfortunately only teach what they have been taught. "When you combine the fluid movements of jujutsu and the hard kicks of karate with submission holds and boxing punches and jabs, you've created a whole new style," he says. "That's real mixed martial arts."

Strategies

Although some fighters throw front and side kicks in NHB matches, Miletich does not believe they are the most effective techniques for the sport. "To execute either of those kicks, you have to exert a lot of energy," he says. "You have to weigh that against your opponent's stamina. You may get more from that energy if you save it for later in the bout. Those kicks are also easier for an experienced fighter to grab. And if you miss your target, you are in trouble fast. You've given your opponent the chance to [improve] his position, close the distance and move in quickly."

While Miletich thinks point-sparring matches provide good training experience in karate, he sees pros and cons when it comes to mixed martial arts. "Point sparring gives you a chance to perfect some important skills and techniques—like speed and agility and how to get in and out without being hit," he says. "But the real downside of using this type of training for fighting—whether you have to fight in the street to defend yourself or willingly get in the cage to fight—is that you don't learn to punch through your target. It's tap-tap-tap. There's no power there. You always have to punch through your target. Punching is a perishable technique. You must keep practicing."

Although Miletich stays in shape year-round and works out every day, he adopts an intensive eight-week workout schedule prior to each fight, knowing he needs to maintain his mental and physical sharpness for bouts with world-class opponents.

Miletich has triumphed in five UFC events. He currently owns the lightweight title.

"Conditioning must be an important part of every martial artist's training," he says. From experience, he knows that the best strategy against a superior fighter is to "weather the storm" for the first few minutes of the match, then take the fight to him as he tires. "You can't do that if you're gassed in 30 seconds," he says.

Instead of going all-out in the first few minutes of a match, Miletich prefers to let his opponent punch himself out and then attack him when he's tired.

Even with the best conditioning and training, Miletich sees injury as an almost inevitable part of a fighter's career. Interestingly, he says injuries are more likely to occur during training than during an actual cage match. "If you take a hard shot to the head in a training session, your partner will most likely let up on you a little," he says. "But if you take a hard body shot, he might try to take advantage and come in with a couple of low kicks."

There is value to practicing while injured, Miletich says. "If you can hide your injury from your training partner, you're more likely to pull it off with an opponent. One secret that all fighters learn early is not to let your opponent know you are hurt—or tired. You have to focus beyond the injury."

He still remembers the words of a former strength and conditioning coach: "Just go out there and fight. You can deal with the pain later."

When deciding how to approach a new opponent, Miletich starts by judging how he reacts to takedown shots. "If the guy is a stand-up fighter, I might come in with some crisp, sharp jabs to the head," he says. "And I want him to respect those jabs. When he tries to protect his head, I go in for the takedown. Many mixed martial artists will go for the guillotine too soon. This is where patience pays off—and a top-notch fighter knows that. You always fight for position and angles first, cutting off his offensive weapons so you get ahead. From there, he is always playing catch-up. He gets physically and mentally exhausted while trying to figure out what to do next."

Philosophies

Many martial artists are taught to fight by the principle of *yin-yang*—oppose a hard stylist with soft-style techniques, fight a linear fighter with circular techniques, confront a striker with grappling and a grappler with striking, etc. Miletich, however, does not abide by that philosophy. Although he agrees with the general principle, he prefers to beat his opponent using what he is best at so he can impose his will on the other man, thereby crushing him mentally. "But to do that, you have to decide if you have the confidence and skills in those areas," he says.

The type of opponent Miletich fears the most is the one who is dangerous on his feet and on the mat. The opponent is also intelligent, adaptive, thinks ahead and can dictate the pace of the bout.

How does Miletich want such an opponent to see him? "I want him to fear me in all positions, to know that I can take him down from all positions. This makes him tense, and he will wear himself down faster. And I want him to know that I can win because I have outworked him."

And how does he see himself? "I know that when I enter the cage, I am testing my skills against another man's to see who is the best fighter on that particular day," Miletich says. "I've done everything I can do to be that fighter, and now it's time to relax, focus and just do my best. It's a test of our human spirit, will and endurance.

"When the fight is over, we shake hands and go home. And at the end of the day, if I can look at the man in the mirror and say I've done my best whether I've won or lost, I'm happy."

But, of course, he'd rather win.

The key to victory in no-holds-barred fighting, says Miletich, is performing so many repetitions of your striking and grappling techniques that they become second nature.

CHUCK LIDDELL
WRESTLES HIS WAY TO THE TOP

by Sara Fogan • Grappling & NHB 2001

Chuck "The Iceman" Liddell is no stranger to no-holds-barred fighting. Boasting a 7-1 NHB record, he was the 2000 International Fighting Championship light-heavyweight champion and veteran of the Ultimate Fighting Championship.

Liddell started training in *koei-kan* karate at age 12 and became interested in wrestling when he was a sophomore in high school. A football coach insisted that any player who did not participate in a winter sport do some wrestling, and Liddell discovered a new calling.

"He thought wrestling was good for football," Liddell recalls. "But I just really liked it, and I wound up being a decent wrestler."

Liddell, 30, continued to practice his stand-up skills and accrued a 20-2 record in kickboxing. He earned a first-degree black belt in koei-kan and a second-degree black belt in "pit *kempo*," a unique style practiced at his *dojo* (training hall). Liddell also trains in *jujutsu*, wrestling, kickboxing and boxing. The lion's share of his competition, however, takes place in the NHB arena.

"I really like mixing everything up," he says. "It's the ultimate sport."

Liddell, who lives in San Luis Obispo, California, currently trains two to three hours a day, six days a week. In addition to running and weightlifting three days a week, the 6-foot-1-inch, 195-pound fighter practices wrestling and stand-up drills. Although he claims he does not significantly change his training regimen before a fight, his prospective opponent's strengths do influence which skills he focuses on when he trains.

"Some days, I'll work harder on my wrestling," Liddell says. "For the mixed-martial arts, maybe I'll stress one thing more than the other things, depending on who I'm fighting."

Like most other up-and-coming martial artists, Liddell works out with a variety of opponents to gain experience going against different martial arts and techniques. His regular training partner is Scott Adams, but he also exchanges kicks and punches with John "The Train" Hackleman, a world-class kickboxer. To hone his ground skills, Liddell rolls with jujutsu-stylist John Lewis, a black belt under Gene LeBell. Liddell also regularly works out with the California Polytechnic Institute wrestling team. Despite the geographic distance between them, Liddell trains with UFC middleweight champ Tito Ortiz. "We are regular training partners when we've got fights coming up," Liddell says.

When he is not preparing for his own fights, Liddell coaches other martial artists for their upcoming bouts. He also runs and co-owns the SLO Kickboxing gym in San Luis Obispo.

After a significant winning streak—which included a UFC XVII victory over Noe Hernandez and a unanimous decision over No. 1-ranked *vale tudo* champion Jose "Pele" Landi-Jons in the IFC—Liddell injured his ankle in December 1999 while training with Ortiz. He did not fight again for seven months. However, he never stopped training and is looking forward to an upcoming UFC bout.

"My goal in fighting is to fight," Liddell explains. "The fights alone motivate me; competition motivates me. That's what helps me train hard and stay at the level I'm at."

Skilled in wrestling, kickboxing, karate and jujutsu, Chuck Liddell is a staunch advocate of cross-training in different arts with different opponents.

MARCO RUAS
The King of the Streets Is on the Road Back

by Stephen Quadros • Grappling and NHB 2001

Many athletes do not realize greatness until they are confronted with adversity in the ring and in life, for that is what reveals one's true character. Marco Ruas has faced challenges that would have broken most men—everything from fighters in his home country refusing to fight him to career-threatening injuries. But he is a survivor. He triumphed in Brazil and the United States.

His success, both as a trainer and a fighter, is proof that he is a true pioneer of vale tudo fighting. His style, called Ruas Vale Tudo, has produced several noteworthy champions, including Pedro Rizzo, Renato "Babalu" Sobral and

Marco Ruas (left) has been called one of the most complete fighters alive. He possesses extensive stand-up and ground-fighting skills and has used them to defeat some of the toughest opponents around.

Alexandre Barros. A native of Rio de Janeiro, Ruas now runs a gym in Laguna Niguel, California, where he will continue to churn out champions.

Ruas, who is 39 years old, began training in judo at 13 with an uncle who is a black belt, Vinicio Ruas. The gym where he learned the grappling art also taught taekwondo, capoeira and boxing. Young Marco soaked up knowledge like a sponge and excelled in boxing, winning his first eight-man tournament as a 14-year-old middleweight at 160 pounds. He later graduated to muay Thai under Flavio Molina. Ruas compiled an undefeated record in kickboxing and lost only one boxing match. Soon he was perfecting his ground fighting by learning luta livre with Fausto Brunocilla and lifelong friend Roberto Leitao. In Brazil, luta livre began to rival jujutsu, which had always been popular because of the accomplishments of the Gracie family. This rivalry occasionally spilled over into street confrontations and dojo wars.

—S.Q.

Black Belt: How did the *luta livre* vs. *jujutsu* rivalry begin?

Marco Ruas: I think it was in 1983, when a *taekwondo* guy named Mario—Flavio Molina's brother-in-law—beat Charles Gracie in a street fight. Mario was a very tough street fighter, but Charles told everybody he was jumped by many guys, not just Mario. So Rolls Gracie, Charles' brother, took a bunch of students and invaded the taekwondo studio and beat everybody. The police showed up, and there were a lot of problems. Rolls attacked Mario and took him down. Mario put his fingers in Rolls' eyes. All Rolls' students jumped in and kicked Mario. Then Rolls mounted Mario and broke his nose. It was bad for Flavio. He lost a lot of students.

Then Robson Gracie approached some kung fu practitioners to fight in a *vale tudo* event against jujutsu. The problem was that Rolls died from a broken neck in a hang-gliding accident. The kung fu guy told Mario that Robson was looking for guys to fight against jujutsu. Flavio saw the opportunity for revenge in the ring. I wanted to fight, so I told Mario I would fight for him. I had nothing against jujutsu, no problems. I just wanted to fight. So Flavio, Eugenio Tadeu, Marcelo Mendes and I went to Fausto Brunocilla's luta livre school to train on the ground. Fausto told us they should not fight because they needed more time. He said that I would do good because I could box and had good defense on the ground but that they would all lose. He told us to cancel the fight. But Helio Gracie wouldn't let us cancel. He did not want to give us time to train. He would not change the date. Marcelo pulled out, but Flavio, Eugenio and I accepted. The rules said there would be no more than an 11-pound weight difference. I was 174

Ruas claims his protégé, Pedro Rizzo, is the most skilled NHB fighter in the world. Rizzo has already chalked up a string of impressive victories in the UFC—most recently over Dan Severn.

pounds at the time. The guy I was supposed to fight was a jujutsu black belt named Fred Bomba. But Fred did not want to fight me because he felt I had too much experience. So they changed my opponent to Fernando Pinduka, a much heavier black belt under Carlson Gracie. I complained, "Why will Fred not fight me?" They said Fred was out partying too much.

BB: So who changed the opponent from Bomba to Pinduka?

Ruas: Robson changed it. Pinduka outweighed me by 22 pounds. The fight ended in a draw after three five-minute rounds. Eugenio won his match with strikes. He held the *gi* and punched while standing and on the ground in the guy's guard. The jujutsu fighter then took off his gi but got beat anyway. The jujutsu guy's corner threw in the towel. Flavio lost from punches while he was mounted by Marcelo Behring, a student of Rickson Gracie.

BB: Rickson was becoming prominent in Brazil at the same time all this was happening. Did you two ever meet?

Ruas: Everybody thought I would lose to Pinduka, but I didn't. After that fight, Rickson, who was there, looked at me and said, "Good." A few years later, Flavio Molina went on TV and said that luta livre was the best and that Rickson had never proved anything. So Helio Gracie, Rickson Gracie and Marcelo Behring went to the luta livre gym and Rickson challenged Zulu. I said, "Zulu? He's a fake fighter." He would sometimes fight real fights and sometimes fake fights for money.

Rickson got angry. Carlos Brunocilla was trying to instigate a showdown between Rickson and me. He called me on the phone and said that Rickson was going to challenge me. So I went to the gym and saw Rickson, Helio and Marcelo Behring. Helio was very nice and said, "Oh, Marco, how are you?"

I told Rickson, "I came here because Brunocilla said you wanted to challenge me. So you want to fight me? I'm ready to fight you." But Rickson said he did not come to challenge me. He said he respected me and I had proved I was a good fighter. Rickson said he wanted to fight someone else from luta livre. I had three fights in vale tudo after that and won all of them. Then I moved to the United States.

BB: What's new in your professional life?

Ruas: My gym. I am very happy here in Laguna Niguel because, among other reasons, it's close to the beach. Every day I get more students and show them Ruas Vale Tudo. Some of my students are fighting and showing good results. And my knee is much better. I had surgery in April. I was very depressed when I was hurt. My recovery is going well, and I expect to get in the ring again and fight—maybe next April in Coliseum 2001 [a rising NHB

Marco Ruas faces Pedro Rizzo (1). Rizzo shoots in for a leg, and Ruas underhooks his arms (2). After Ruas drops to his knees (3), he frees his trapped leg (4). He then repositions his right thigh alongside the opponent's head (5) and his left leg around his right shoulder (6). Ruas then rolls the other man and squeezes with his legs (7).

show in Japan]. I am training very hard and I feel 100 percent. Babalu and Pedro Rizzo worked out with me recently, and they were surprised that I had recovered so quickly. The ligaments are fine. I will fight again.

BB: In your last Ultimate Fighting Championship fight with Maurice Smith, you were forced to retire after round one because of your knee. Was it injured before the bout?

Ruas: Yes. My fight with Maurice was the main event. I signed a contract and was under a great deal of stress because I did not want to pull out at the last minute and say I hurt my knee a few days before the fight. Now I realize I was wrong. I should have pulled out. This was the second time the knee had caused me to lose. The first time was in Japan against Alexander Otsuka [in PRIDE]. On that occasion, I hurt my knee training with Mark Kerr one week before.

BB: Exactly how did that happen?

Ruas: We were working out at Takada Dojo. Kerr asked me to show him an armbar. He was in my guard. I held his arm and passed my leg in front of his face, and the knee went out. It made a loud noise. Bang! I started taking lots of really strong Brazilian anti-inflammatory drugs. This made me very tired and my arms very heavy. I couldn't throw any kicks because I was worried that my knee would go out. The PRIDE people did not have an opponent for me so they put in Otsuka, who was a pro wrestler. He had

As the "King of the Streets" can attest, leg locks are devastating in the ring or on the pavement. This is why they are an important component of Ruas Vale Tudo.

never had a real vale tudo fight before. But now that I'm healthy, Otsuka won't give me a rematch. That's not fair. I gave him a chance, and he got a big name from beating me, but now he won't give me a chance.

BB: Would you like a rematch with Smith, too?

Ruas: Of course. I want to fight him again. I did not fight in that match. They had already sold T-shirts and posters and had paid for my flight and Pedro and Roberto Leitao's flights. I thought I had to fight. I didn't want to get sued.

BB: How is Ruas Vale Tudo different from other NHB systems?

Ruas: For me, the most important thing with Ruas Vale Tudo is the family. The guys—Pedro, Roberto and the students—all support each other. Everyone helps his or her teammates. Nowadays, a lot of people are training right—with the proper cross-training. Teams like Ken Shamrock's Lion's Den and Pat Miletich's team are cross-training. But I created this system a long time ago, when I combined wrestling, submissions, boxing and

Ruas often puts his boxing background to good use in NHB competition.

107

kickboxing. I think I was one of the first to put all these elements together. Now you have people like Maurice Smith and Frank Shamrock, who have formed an alliance to share knowledge.

BB: Your student, Pedro Rizzo, is regarded as one of the best fighters in mixed martial arts. He competes primarily in the UFC. Does he have plans to try his hand in other organizations—like PRIDE?

Ruas: Pedro is happy in the UFC. His contract is still good for another six months. He wants to fight for the UFC title again. [Rizzo lost a decision to Kevin Randleman in a recent title fight.] Randy Couture has not fought in the UFC for a while and he got a shot at the title. I think Pedro is the best NHB fighter in the world. He's the most complete, with good kickboxing skills and good defense on the ground. No one has really seen what he can do on the ground.

BB: What happened when Pedro fought Randleman?

Ruas: The problem was in his mind. About two weeks before the fight, while he was training in Brazil, he got a big cut on his eyebrow. I told him if he pulled out, it would be difficult to fight for the title again. I said it was better for him to honor his commitment and fight. But he was worried about the cut and if it started bleeding that Big John McCarthy would stop the fight. So he was not aggressive and fought too defensively. Then, after Kevin accidentally head-butted him, he complained to me in the corner that he couldn't see anything. I told him to hold the fight and try to maintain his position. I think Pedro is much better than Randleman.

Because Ruas possesses an extensive muay Thai background, his art—Ruas Vale Tudo—contains numerous Thai techniques, such as the straight knee thrust (left) and inside thigh kick (right).

We want a rematch.

BB: Pedro has a teammate, Renato "Babalu" Sobral, who is also a heavyweight. It's understood that they will never fight each other. What can Babalu do to excel in the sport in the meantime?

Ruas: Babalu is also a complete fighter. Pedro has helped him with his Thai boxing. He's a really good wrestler. He has more experience because he's had about 15 fights in RINGS [a Japan-based NHB organization]. This is good because it builds confidence. He's a tough guy. Unfortunately I will not be able to be in his corner when he fights Maurice Smith. But Roberto Leitao will be.

BB: Leitao has become a major figure in your organization. Why?

Ruas: Roberto is the best cornerman. He has helped Babalu a lot. He is also a good friend.

BB: Alexandre Barros is another champion who represents Ruas Vale Tudo. He won a very tough International Vale Tudo Championship lightweight tournament in August 1999 and recently went the distance with Matt Hughes, the wrestler who many feel is the world's best lightweight NHB fighter. What's he up to?

Ruas: The fight with Matt Hughes we took on short notice. We only had two weeks to prepare. Hughes is a very tough guy, the best in the division. The Hughes fight was in World Extreme Fighting. Alexandre was supposed to fight LaVerne Clark in the next WEF, but the WEF is no more. Alexandre was training hard but didn't fight. I know how frustrating this is. I am trying to negotiate for him to fight in King of the Cage.

BB: Is there anything else you would like to say to the readers of *Black Belt?*

Ruas: I get a lot of e-mails that ask, "Marco, when are you fighting again?" My knee is much better, and I'm training hard. I want to fight again and win for myself, my family and my fans. I will give my best.

MARIO SPERRY ON THE
STREET EFFECTIVENESS OF JUJUTSU

by John A. Goldstein • Photo by Marcelo Alonso • Grappling & NHB 2001

In the past few years, the grappling arts have proved to be among the most effective styles in mixed-martial arts competition. The success of Brazilian *jujutsu,* wrestling and similar styles in the reality-combat arena is the main reason for grappling's surge in popularity. Such events have shown that fighters who know how to grapple have a better chance of winning than fighters who don't.

Brazilian jujutsu is perhaps the most popular grappling system in North America, thanks primarily to Royce Gracie's three Ultimate Fighting Championship titles. Many martial artists believe it is the most realistic approach to street defense one can find today. Along with its tournament triumphs, Brazilian jujutsu is also experiencing incredible commercial success in the United States as thousands of students flock to classes and seminars to learn the techniques that have enabled fighters to win events like the UFC, the World Combat Championship and Extreme Fighting.

Although Brazilian jujutsu may appear to be a martial artist's dream come true, things aren't always what they seem.

Jose Mario Sperry, Brazil's heavyweight jujutsu champion, believes that jujutsu students in the United States may not be learning the street-lethal martial art they think they are. Sperry claims that most of the instructors currently teaching Brazilian jujutsu in the United States are concentrating too much on competition.

"The majority of the Brazilian-jujutsu instructors in America are teaching sport jujutsu," Sperry says. "Americans must understand that sport jujutsu may not be the most effective method of self-defense for the street."

He points out that although sport jujutsu is not necessarily effective on the street, it serves an important function because it enables people to participate in competitive grappling without the risk of injury. He warns, however, that if students are not properly taught the differences between the street and sport versions of the art, they may be left with a false sense of security.

"If they try [sport-jujutsu] techniques in a real fight, they are going to be in for a big shock," Sperry says. "These techniques won't work. Everything from the takedown to the finish of the fight is different [in self-defense]."

Sperry likens sport jujutsu to the fancy martial arts techniques used in movies. "They look great but have no place in a street fight," he explains. "When you compete at the sport-jujutsu level, you use certain positions in a very flamboyant way."

Sperry points to the guard position: "In a jujutsu tournament, you want to pull your opponent into the guard because it enables you to use your legs and perform some really exotic reversals and obtain points. But in a street fight, being on your back is very dangerous, and the guard should only be used if you get into trouble and lose your positioning. If you end up on your back, you need to get out very quickly because a strong opponent can do great damage to you inside your guard."

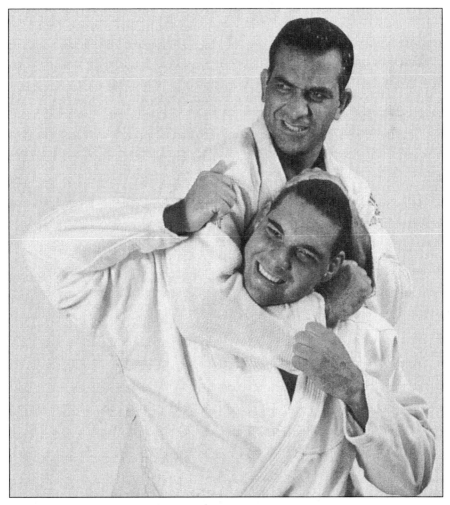

Although many Brazilian-jujutsu techniques function as well on the street as in the ring, Mario Sperry (choking) says many American students are learning only the sporting aspect of the art.

Sperry certainly understands what it takes to win in sport jujutsu and reality combat. He was a convincing winner at 1997's Reality Superfighting show, and he won the heavyweight division at the 1996 and 1997 World Brazilian Jiu-Jitsu Championships in Rio de Janeiro. However, he claims that success in the ring does not necessarily translate into success in reality fighting. And because many Brazilian fighters focus solely on tournaments, they lack the skills needed to properly teach self-defense to their students.

One of the biggest problems practitioners will face when making the transition from sport to the street is in the area of takedowns, Sperry says. "The takedowns used in a street situation are drastically different [from those used in sport jujutsu]. If you think you are going to use a fancy hip throw or double-leg takedown on the street, things may not go as planned. This type of takedown will not work against a good street fighter. To effectively take a person to the ground on the street, you need to first drive him up against a wall, car or something similar. Then you have your opponent in a very vulnerable position."

Sperry notes that when you force an opponent back against a wall or vehicle, he cannot sprawl to avoid a takedown. It is also difficult for him to punch effectively from this position because he does not have the leverage or space necessary for a strong blow, he adds.

"Having your opponent in this position utilizes the same principles as being mounted on your opponent," he says. "When an opponent is pushed up against a wall, he cannot draw back his punch, or kick or strike with any real force."

"This is the time you can do real damage if you know how," he continues. "If you keep him immobilized, use head butts and continue to punish him, eventually he will practically throw himself down on the ground just to try to get away," Sperry says.

RICKSON GRACIE'S FIGHTING PHILOSOPHIES

by Rickson Gracie • Grappling & NHB 2001

To be a complete fighter, you have to know more than just one finishing hold or technique. The best fighters have a variety of techniques in their arsenal. They have more at their disposal than just one armbar or choke. The better the fighter, the more techniques he possesses.

In addition to this, a good fighter is able to adapt to whatever situation he finds himself in and take advantage of his opponent's mistakes. A good fighter capitalizes on the opportunities his opponent presents to him.

Many times you have a favorite technique, but it is not always possible to get into position to use it during a competition. This is especially true if your opponent is aware of what technique you are positioning yourself for. When you are pitted against a strong fighter who is 100 percent committed to denying you that move, the contest becomes a physical fight, and I don't believe in physical fights. I believe in strategic fights.

Instead of trying to pursue a technique that your opponent is completely committed to stopping, you should look to exploit his weakness, whatever that may be. You should try to keep yourself well-tuned for all situations—defense, offense and finishing. You must take advantage of the easiest way to achieve your goal. You never know how long it's going to take to execute a specific move that your opponent is already aware of. Therefore, go for the weakness—the opening, if you will.

Rickson Gracie (right, performing a kneebar on a training partner) says he has no favorite technique. Rather, he is happy to use whatever is necessary to defeat his opponent.

113

Another point regarding preferred techniques: I personally don't have a favorite move. I enjoy a myriad of techniques, including arm, foot and knee locks and chokes of all kinds. When I fight, I use whatever is necessary to win.

Some people say the martial arts are supposed to be defensive in nature. I believe it depends on the martial art and the situation. Some arts stress the offensive—striking first. Others stress using the opponent's offensive energy against him—playing defense.

Those are opposite concepts; how can they exist in the same martial art?

I believe that whether you should play offense or defense depends on whether you're involved in a street fight or a competition. On the street, I'm more than happy to be totally defensive, not committing myself to anything. I make sure that mentally, spiritually and technically I'm prepared to protect myself against whatever might happen. In a competition, however, many times I will try to set up my opponent by committing myself 50 percent to a certain strategy. If he is able to respond to that strategy, then I might cut the action short and do something else.

Although I certainly perform a lot of grappling moves, *jujutsu* gives me the tools and the capacity to understand the striking aspects of a fight. Therefore, I appreciate head butts, elbow strikes, knee strikes, punches and kicks. During many fights, I'm not only fighting from a grappling standpoint, but from a striking one, as well. However, if my opponent is bigger, stronger, quicker and faster than I am, grappling is a good option. In those contests in which my opponent's size and speed are proportional to mine, I would be happy to finish the fight by striking. I'm a warrior who will do whatever is necessary to win.

When it comes to ending a match, I prefer to use a choke over other techniques. This is not to say I won't use other submission methods. But I prefer choking because it's more gentle and humane than the alternatives. A joint lock, for example, is extremely painful and can break an opponent's arm. But he may continue to fight even after something breaks. With a choke, I can maintain a tremendous amount of control and be very effective. And nobody gets hurt.

KAZUSHI SAKURABA IS
THE KING OF THE WORLD!

by Stephen Quadros • Photo by Robert W. Young • Grappling & NHB 2001

Kazushi Sakuraba is the biggest name ever to come out of the Japanese no-holds-barred circuit. Although he has an extensive wrestling background, it is his unconventional strikes, pre-fight humor and all-around showmanship that help him stand out more than that of any other competitor in the under-200-pound division. He rose to the top of the no-holds-barred world with victories over the greatest names in the sport: Vitor Belfort, Ebenezer Fontes Braga, Carlos Newton, Vernon "Tiger" White, Marcus "Conan" Silveira, and Royler, Royce and Renzo Gracie. Sakuraba has shattered the misconception that professional wrestlers can't win real fights.

Black Belt: How old were you when you started training in the martial arts?

Kazushi Sakuraba: Fifteen.

BB: What was your first style?

Sakuraba: Wrestling. When I was in high school, I came in second in the nationals. I wrestled in college for four and a half years. I took first place in the freshman league. I was very proud to have beaten Kat Ota, who was a bronze medalist in the 1996 Olympics. After college, I started professional wrestling with the Universal Wrestling Federation International.

BB: What was it like to work with the UWFI?

Playing it as cool as a cucumber in the PRIDE Grand Prix 2000, Kazushi Sakuraba (right) attempts to submit Royce Gracie with a kneebar.

115

Sakuraba: I was 24 when I joined the organization. I was there for three or four years. I don't remember exactly how many fights I had. It was a good experience. I learned submissions and how to punch and kick.

BB: When did you leave pro wrestling and begin competing in real fights?

Sakuraba: December 21, 1997. The opponent was Marcus "Conan" Silveira from the Carlson Gracie team in the UFC Japan four-man heavyweight tournament.

BB: That was a controversial beginning. Silveira outweighed you by at least 40 pounds, yet you blocked most of his punches while you attempted a single-leg takedown. Referee John McCarthy stopped the fight in the middle of the action, awarding Silveira a TKO victory. You and your entourage protested. Do you have anything to add to that?

Sakuraba: I believe it was the referee's fault. It was a misjudgment. Of course the first punch landed, but after that, I defended myself.

BB: After the match, you got emotional and threw down your mouthpiece. Then you attempted to grab the announcer's microphone and refused to leave the octagon.

Sakuraba: I didn't leave the ring because my cornermen wouldn't let me leave. If it was up to me, I would have left. [Note: It proved to be a wise decision not to leave. On the other end of the tournament bracket, David "Tank" Abbott had decisioned Yoji Anjo, but Abbott broke his hand in the process. Neither fighter was fit to continue, so in an unprecedented move, the UFC overturned the Silveira/Sakuraba TKO. It was deemed a no-contest, and the two men met again in the finals. Sakuraba executed an armbar and made the big Brazilian tap.]

BB: In your *vale tudo* career, you have fought some of the best Brazilian-*jujutsu* fighters: Royce Gracie, Royler Gracie, Renzo Gracie, Vitor Belfort and Allan Goes. You defeated them all—except Goes, whom you fought to a draw. What problems did those opponents present?

Sakuraba: When I fight, I make the opponent fight my style, not his style. I watch a video of my opponent, but I don't make a strategy for the individual.

BB: Of all the Brazilians you have fought, who was the toughest?

Sakuraba: Allan Goes. In that fight, I fought his style, not mine. I think I lost that fight.

BB: Would you like a rematch with him?

Sakuraba: I'd like a rematch. However, I can only fight four or five times a year, so I would rather fight someone I have not fought before.

BB: What do you think about Frank Shamrock?

Sakuraba: As a person, I don't know anything about him. As a fighter, I think he is very good on the ground and very good standing. He's also very handsome. (laughs) He's much better looking than I am. (more laughs)

BB: You defeated Royler, Royce and Renzo. Would you now consider fighting Rickson Gracie, the man who is widely regarded as the family champion?

Sakuraba: No. Because in order to get him in the ring, the promoter has to pay far too much money, and no one makes a profit. Of course, a fight is unpredictable, so I really don't know what would happen.

BB: In your fights, you occasionally do things that are considered unorthodox, even flamboyant. For example, you'll use a spinning back kick or jump up and land on the other person. Why is it important for you to be entertaining?

Sakuraba: I don't do it to be entertaining. I do it to surprise my opponent.

BB: In the PRIDE Grand Prix 2000 semifinals, you faced the punching power of Igor Vovchanchyn, who has won five eight-man NHB tournaments. What was that like?

Sakuraba: His punches hurt. They were very heavy.

BB: Is Nobuhiko Takada, the famous pro wrestler whom Rickson Gracie twice defeated, your teacher?

Sakuraba: Not my teacher, but the president of the Takada Dojo [where I train]. He is also my senior.

BB: Why hasn't Takada been as successful in NHB fighting as you have been?

Sakuraba: No comment. (smiles)

BB: What message would you like to deliver to your American fans?

Sakuraba: I will train even harder, so please watch PRIDE. If you are a martial artist, keep training. Don't give up, and you will become strong.

117

THE ULTIMATE GRAPPLER
AND THE ULTIMATE STRIKER
Gene LeBell and Benny Urquidez Reveal
How They Became Martial Arts Legends

by Tony Salzano • Grappling and NHB 2001

*T*he upheaval caused by the Ultimate Fighting Championship and other reality-based competitions has focused attention on several new concepts in fighting strategy and techniques. Martial artists have reacted with everything from curiosity to rage.

Regardless of individual opinion, one concept has become clear: In real fighting, there are basically two types of fighters—grapplers and strikers. This crucial observation inspired this article—an interview with Gene LeBell, the "Ultimate Grappler," and Benny Urquidez, the "Ultimate Striker."

LeBell is highly regarded by martial artists and has become a living legend. How does a person beat a guy like him in a match?

"You don't," says Pancrase champion and UFC VI superfight winner Ken Shamrock. "A guy like that is so tough that you're not going to intimidate him. He's so strong that you're not going to knock him out. Basically, to beat a guy like Gene LeBell, you have to cheat. You either have to come up from behind him and get lucky to get a choke, or you have to kick him in the groin."

Black Belt: Do you fight a grappler differently from a striker?

Gene LeBell: You always go for what you consider his weakness. You attack or counterattack his weakness, no matter if he's a wrestler or karate man.

BB: If your opponent is built strong on top, you go down for his legs?

LeBell: Yes. Everybody has a different weakness. Some are jabbers, some are plodders, some are fast movers. You attack them all differently. Every martial artist has weaknesses, some more than others. And every art has weaknesses, and that includes judo and wrestling.

BB: Can you give an example of taking advantage of the other man's weakness?

LeBell: If you're fighting a boxer, he has no defense below his waist; you take him down and then it's the best wrestler [who wins]. You play your own game, not his. A boxer can't force you to stand up, but you sure can force him to lie down.

BB: Are certain techniques more effective for certain body types, like a 5-foot-4-inch, 130-pound man who has to fight a big, strong wrestler like

Ken Shamrock or Dan Severn?

LeBell: The first thing you do if you run into a Shamrock or Severn is get out of his reach fast. You must live to fight another day. But if you can't get out of there, you can open your hand so you have a four-inch longer reach, and the toughest guy is the one who can take out the other man's eyes first. The nerve endings are so close to the brain that you don't even have to take the eye out—you can "dot" it. If you get a thumb in the eye, it can be all over.

BB: No one can resist an eye strike?

LeBell: Right. The ultimate martial artist is a guy who can humiliate his opponent instead of hurt him. Benny Urquidez can hit you 100 times in a minute and kill you with any one of them, or just humiliate you like that and not hurt you. The thing I admire about Benny is that not only is he a classic in his field and a legend in his own time, but he's also an

LeBell's most precious bit of advice for cross-trainers: The best way to defeat an opponent—no matter which art he practices—is to capitalize on his weaknesses.

outstanding grappler. People don't know he's a grappler because when they see him, he's doing full-body contact. Grapplers should also know how to block, bob and weave. You should learn all arts so you can defend against all arts.

BB: What should students look for in an art, an instructor and a school?

LeBell: If you're going to talk the talk, walk the walk. The man that enjoys himself will [learn] better. When I say learn, I mean ....

BB: ... that it becomes second nature in a real fight?

LeBell: Good. How many people have taken grappling or karate, and when they get in a real fight, they start swinging [wildly] with their arms? Make sure the techniques work—whatever art you practice—and that they become second nature, like walking or eating strawberry shortcake.

BB: What does it take to be a great fighter?

LeBell: Practice and conditioning. To get good, you have to be in condition. This is critical. Also, full-body contact and sparring against an opponent who resists are very important.

BB: How many times a week should a person work out?

LeBell: The more you work out, the better you get. The harder you work out in any vocation or avocation, the better you get.

BB: And the length of each workout?

LeBell: It depends on your teacher. Some work you for a half-hour, some for an hour, some for an hour and a half. My students are not commercial fighters, and they're usually all champions and contenders in their own right. I like to work them long and hard for six hours. When they call me a sadistic so-and-so under their breath, I consider it a compliment.

BB: Do you have any special techniques for fighting a guy who is much bigger and heavier?

LeBell: Yeah, a gun. Size is not the criterion; it's the amount of ability the size has. If a guy is much bigger, you must estimate his ability, and you can never be completely accurate. If it's [Mike] Tyson, you fight him differently than a guy who just got out of an iron lung or who's just big and eats a lot. Sometimes it takes years before your technique becomes second nature. There are no shortcuts to success.

BB: Do you have a favorite technique?

LeBell: I like a series of techniques. If a man does not have a weapon, he has only five units: two—

BB: —two arms, two legs and a head to attack you with. If he's beside you, he has two weapons: one arm and one leg. When you're behind him, he doesn't have any.

LeBell: You're my man.

BB: I've seen your videos and read your books. I think *Grappling Master* and *The Handbook of Judo* form the bible of grappling.

LeBell: Good. The first and most important thing in self-defense is to not get hurt—to save your butt. If a guy has a tremendous advantage and you're the underdog, get out of there and come back and fight when you're not the underdog.

BB: What is more important: speed or strength?

LeBell: It's a combination of both. If you're strong but you move in slow motion, you're not going to hit anything.

Photo by Fernando Escovar

BB: Do you fight differently for self-defense as opposed to competition?

LeBell: Yes. In self-defense, if two or more guys are attacking, one could blindside you while you are grappling with his friend. You'd have to use full-body-contact striking and grappling—such as Benny does.

BB: Are there any other karate men you like?

LeBell: There's a lot of them. For starters, Joe Lewis, Bill "Superfoot" Wallace and Chuck Norris. They're my heroes, along with Benny. I like Bill Wallace because

Demonstrating just how hard it is to get away from his pro-wrestling roots, LeBell picks up Armando Guerrero for a body slam.

he's a scratch golfer and rides motorcycles. Joe Lewis I like because in a commercial he used my three-finger grip, plus he eats raw meat—both of which are my inventions. Joe is also a fantastic karate man who likes to grapple. I always admire martial artists who do other arts besides their specialty. I like Bill also because he eats hamburgers for breakfast, lunch and dinner.

BB: Who are your favorite grapplers?

LeBell: Lou Thesz and Karl Gotch. Karl taught me, also. He would just put his hands on you, and it'd hurt.

BB: You are a big fan of reality-based combat. Why do great, experienced fighters sometimes forget the simple things like using the finger spread, grabbing the groin or using the "half Boston crab" when held in the guard?

LeBell: Bad training or bad trainers.

Benny Urquidez is often compared to the most famous martial artist of all time—Bruce Lee. One reason is that Urquidez possesses the fighting qualities and attributes Lee had. Another is that, just as the "Little Dragon" was a legend in his time, so is "The Jet."

Most spectators are impressed whenever they see Urquidez fight—not just by the fact that he always wins but also by how quickly and firmly he establishes his superiority over his opponent. He plays a "kickboxing chess game" with his opponent, often establishing psychological dominance over him—sometimes even before the opening bell.

BB: What is the key to winning a fight?

Benny Urquidez: To fight for the right reason. My purpose for fighting is for sport—to perform if it's not self-defense. I never hit anybody out of bitterness, anger or hatred. I hit them for the right reason. Ten guys [may have] the same knowledge, but each responds differently under pressure. Some are great, some not. It's how you control your emotions. I don't care what you know; if you can't control it under pressure, it's not any good. If you're mad, frustrated or afraid, it doesn't work. You have to be in control of your emotions. That's the key.

BB: Do you fight a striker differently from a grappler?

Urquidez: Absolutely. If somebody kicks and punches at me, I redirect the movement, either clockwise or counterclockwise, to get away from his movement. If he comes forward, I move at a 45-degree angle; that way I'm out of his line of fire. From that point, as soon as he strikes, I parry it or deflect it. For every mistake he makes, I take advantage of it. Usually a grappler needs to grab hold of me first. The key to avoiding that is to keep something in his face. Most grapplers are not used to seeing a fist come at their face, so they duck their head and reach to grab your legs. I like to go side to side, so as long as I have my hand in his face, I'm blinding him. From that point, I have my choice: jump on his back, side-kick his joints or throw an uppercut, since he can't see what I'm doing. I can also use elbows and knees to the face. The problem is that, when it's happening quickly, you have to be able to respond to it. If you have to think about it, it's too late. It's a matter of fear response, zero response and fine-tuning your senses.

BB: Is sidestepping important when someone charges?

Urquidez: Absolutely, deflecting his power and strength away from you.

To avoid an attack, "The Jet" prefers to sidestep the blow before countering with a vicious kick or punch of his own.

BB: As a martial arts legend who has been fighting for decades, what do you think of self-appointed masters who create "new" arts in their own name?

Urquidez: Let me put it this way: You can only kick, punch and throw so many ways. I don't care what your belt rank is; it doesn't tell if you're good or bad. It tells how much knowledge you should have. So everyone who makes up their own style is trying to fool the public. But the public is too sharp now; they can only be fooled so much and for so long. When you have people making up their own style, they're trying to get money from the public. We're all here to learn; the man upstairs put us here to learn about ourselves.

BB: How should a striker fight a taller and heavier opponent?

Urquidez: When someone is taller than me, I get out my ax and start to chop. I chop his knees, calves and thighs. I'm a strong believer in taking out the front leg. If I do that, you can't stand on it; and if you can't stand on it, you can't punch, kick or grab me because the front leg is usually the leg needed to throw force. So I don't care if the guy is 3 feet tall, 6 feet tall or 9 feet tall. Once I have his front leg beaten up where he can't stand on it, I have the advantage. With a huge fellow like that, you can't let him grab you. Any big man automatically thinks if he's stronger, the first thing he wants to do is grab you, squeeze your head, pop it and so forth. A smaller guy taking him down or hurting him is his biggest fear.

BB: These days, a lot of martial artists practice only self-defense techniques that end a fight instantly.

Urquidez: Good. It's rough anywhere you go. The stronger you are, the more knowledge you have and the more humble you become.

BB: Some experts have compared fighting with a chess game. Do you play chess?

Urquidez: Absolutely. I play a physical game of chess. I use it because I believe there are—

BB: —two types of fighters: chess players and checkers players?

Urquidez: Right. A checkers player will take two hits to give you one, while a chess player will take none and give you four, five and six. I've survived 23 years holding the title for that reason.

BB: To be proficient at fighting, how often should a martial artist train?

Urquidez: Basically every day.

BB: With not even one day off?

Urquidez: Nope ... well, other than Sunday. Sunday is actually my, should I say, my junk-food day.

BB: In your book, you said one day off a week was allowed.

Urquidez: Yeah, so Sunday I usually spend with the family, and if my body craves sugar, I eat sugar. If I crave salt, I eat salt.

BB: Where did you learn that?

Urquidez: I've been blessed, very fortunate, to go around the world and work out with a lot of masters—top people at what they do. I've worked out with all types of people, so I've formulated [a list of] all the do's and don'ts—all the things you can have and all the things you should keep away from.

When fighting a bigger opponent, Urquidez likes to take out his "ax" and start chopping with roundhouse kicks to the legs.

BB: How long should a workout last?

Urquidez: People can train for three hours and do nothing, and others can train for five minutes and be drenched. So it's not so much how long it is; it's what you put into it.

BB: On the subject of speed vs. strength, would you say one is more important when facing a striker or a grappler?

Urquidez: I'd rather be someone that's real quick and hit you constantly, because it's not how hard you hit—it's how right you hit. Also, I can carve, I can snap at you. It's like a whip—damage is done at the end of it. That's what does the tearing, just like a jab. The end of the jab is what tears the face. So I can actually cut you up with my hand just by snapping and tearing at you. If I wanted to knock out a puncher, I would actually use my front hand to jab at his eyebrow and cut the top of it so blood ends up in his face.

BB: And then he can't see.

Urquidez: That's it.

BB: Do you approach self-defense and competition differently, or are all the techniques the same?

Urquidez: They're always different. When I jump into the "square jungle," whatever rules they go by are what I go by. But on the street, it's a matter of survival, and the fight doesn't end on the ground. It ends when he can't continue.

BB: Who do you think is the best striker and the best grappler ever?

Urquidez: Well, you can forget who is the best grappler—we all know that one right off the bat.

BB: Is Gene LeBell your first choice?

Urquidez: Well, it's not a choice—that's just it. There's no choice. He stands out. He holds the aces when it comes to grappling. As far as a puncher-striker is concerned, there is a pretty good heavyweight, Stan "The Man" Longinidis, an Australian that they call "Thunder From Down Under." He's got a hell of a strike on him.

TAO OF FRANK SHAMROCK
The Evolution of a No-Holds-Barred Champion Continues

by Josh Gross • November 2002

How many times have you stood on a street corner, unsure of what to do for those 30 seconds that pass before you get the green light to cross? If you've spent much time in the martial arts, you've probably felt compelled to throw a few jab-cross combinations, recall your latest session in the *dojo* or review the techniques you'll need to know for your next belt test. Imagine what that half minute is like for a man who's devoted his life to the martial arts, for a man who views training as a way of life—for a man like Frank Shamrock.

Photo by Rick Hustead

Frank Shamrock (left) has used the past few years to hone his stand-up striking skills under the tutelage of coach Javier Mendez.

Probably the most decorated athlete in the history of the Ultimate Fighting Championship, Shamrock is anything but a typical martial artist. His success in the ring is the result of his mastery of the techniques he's accumulated over the years. His life is like his study of the combat arts: a never-ending struggle to achieve perfection. And he devotes most every waking moment to that pursuit.

"I don't think there's anything that I've perfected, and if I were to say that, I would probably quit studying and begin sliding backward," says Shamrock, who was *Black Belt's* 1998 Full-Contact Fighter of the Year. "The goal—and it's the same in every martial art—is always to do it better, to do it quicker and to do more damage when you're doing it."

When he started out in mixed martial arts, he trained with big brother Ken Shamrock, but those days are long gone. Frank clawed his way to the top of the food chain. A mix of evolution and experimentation may have led him to where he is today, but the learning process is far from over.

Despite a three-year hiatus from the ring that saw him pursue a career in acting after falling out of love with the game that made him a world champion, he continued to study the martial arts. "I felt the urge every day, and I did have to fight it," admits Shamrock, who fought in a 2001 K-1 match during the layoff. "I continued to train and study, but for the most part I just tried to put it out of my mind because I was sure I was done with it."

Not quite. Whether he wanted to step away or not, Shamrock continued to work in an environment at San Jose, California's American Kickboxing Academy that made it virtually impossible to wipe his hands clean of the sport he once dominated. Always the student, he worked with trainer Javier Mendez to improve his stand-up striking game, which, he says, was his weakness for a long time.

"Javier has completely changed everything about my striking," Shamrock says. "Maurice Smith was my original teacher, and he was fabulous. He gave me great techniques. But Javier was able to refine those techniques and make them more powerful, more efficient and, at the same time, allow me to take less damage. Javier is also really good at boxing and coaching boxing. He took my punching to a new level where I could easily stand up with Tito [Ortiz], threaten him there and control that game."

An Evolving Art

The landscape of mixed martial arts has changed dramatically from the days of Royce Gracie and Mark Coleman, Shamrock says. No single

Frank Shamrock's K-1 fight in a nutshell: The 185-pound Shamrock mad-dogs the 176-pound Shannon Rich (1). Shamrock unleashes a few kicks (2), one of which breaks Rich's arm (3). Shamrock paces while the doctor examines him (4). Shamrock wins in 53 seconds (5).

discipline rules the octagon anymore. It's the athletes who followed his lead in cross-training and cardiovascular conditioning that have excelled.

Fans of the sport complain about the dwindling number of submission finishes these days. Some speculate that it's because so many high-level competitors have familiarized themselves with grappling arts such as Brazilian *jujutsu,* judo and submission wrestling. The fact that more people know how to apply a submission also means that more people know how to defend against one.

Shamrock insists that the techniques everyone uses aren't any less effective. However, they are governed by a simple philosophy: Everything works, but nothing works for long. "Everybody gets it, sees it and trains in it, and then you just don't get to use it as much. People are just taking that game and trying to make it more efficient, trying to do more damage, trying to get more setups into the same old thing."

Not one to rest on his laurels, Shamrock is attempting to stay on the cutting edge of an extremely dynamic and fast-changing sport. Because the pursuit of new techniques is primarily fruitless, he focuses his energy on the application and understanding of those skills.

"Everything has been done 10,000 times," he says. "It's just [about looking for a] new approach, a new angle where you try to speed it up or make it more efficient so you're using less energy and getting more results. We're doing the same old techniques over and over, but like science, we're trying to perfect them and make them work in a faster, more efficient, more recognizable [manner]."

When inspiration hits and a new idea jumps into his always-active brain, Shamrock confers with those close to him, hoping they can provide feedback or insight that may not have occurred to him. "I get a theory. OK, maybe this task will work this way or maybe this setup [will work.] And then I share it with five or six people. We all study it, and then they all come back with their own variations. Usually one of us has the right idea or has a technique that is perfected or more efficient."

That open-ended way of thinking has allowed Shamrock and other American Kickboxing Academy fighters to become some of the most exciting competitors in the sport today. The way in which he and his men train has created a gym that consistently produces athletes willing to compete on any level at any pace. Like anything else, however, a trial-and-error philosophy can produce its share of bumps, bruises and bloodied egos. But it's just part of the learning process, Shamrock says. "There have been hundreds of techniques where we thought, 'Hey, this is a great idea,' and it turned out not to be. It's just part of the game. You throw the ball, and sometimes the ball drops and you go, 'Hmm.' Then you pick it back up and do the next thing."

Teacher and Student
Acting was one of those things that made Shamrock go "hmm." That's why he decided to return to the sport that made him famous. The learning process continues. His time away from the spotlight gave him the opportunity to obtain some new skills, primarily stand-up, as well as a chance to return to his roots and streamline older techniques that he may have

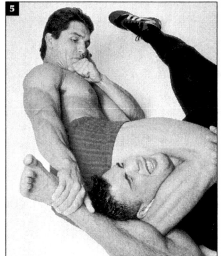

Photos by Todd Feldenstein

The champ in action: Frank Shamrock restrains his opponent's left arm and head (1). The opponent tries to push Shamrock's head back so he can counterattack (2). Shamrock shifts his hips and swings his right leg over the opponent's head and around his neck (3), locking his foot behind his left knee (4). To increase the pressure, he pulls on his foot (5).

taken for granted.

Being able to train up-and-coming fighters has also given him a chance to spread his knowledge to a younger, more athletic breed of fighter than the mixed martial arts have ever seen. Best of all for Shamrock fans, teaching has instilled an even greater understanding of the techniques he carries within himself. "I need to learn it and understand it before I teach it," he says. "But only when I begin teaching it do I really get it, do I really articulate and understand it. That little light goes on and my brain goes, Now you got it."

When the time comes for him to play the student, Shamrock has, through thousands of hours on the mat and in the gym, refined the way he learns. "I have found that I have to separate myself from the technique and look at it from a third-person perspective to grasp what's going on," he says. "I've trained in so many different areas and studied so many different things that the techniques themselves all seem to be the same; there's just better and more efficient ways to do them. So I have to break down what I already know, look at it objectively and simplify it—to make it quicker and more efficient."

There's no doubt that the martial arts, like life, provide a limitless amount of information to absorb. If a man like Shamrock can attest to even now gaining knowledge on a daily basis, that may make the experience of some weekend warriors seem absolutely daunting.

One step at a time, though. While most of us are interested in positioning our bodies in the proper stance or correctly performing an armbar from the guard, Shamrock is obsessed with refining his skills to perfection. Yet in the disciplines he pursues, evolution occurs at an amazing pace, and learning is less about specific techniques than about gaining an understanding of what he needs to do to have his hand raised when it's all said and done.

"The things I was taught when I first started are not the things I teach now because those techniques have evolved," he says. "So the style I trained in is no longer the style we teach. Everything has changed—the knowledge, the theories, the ideas. They're still basically the same techniques; we've just refined the approach to utilizing them."

At his core, though, Frank Shamrock is—physically and mentally—a martial artist. And like any normal practitioner, he doesn't feel silly when he breaks out into a bit of shadowboxing while standing on a street corner.

Shamrock on Jujutsu

"No-holds-barred fighting now is a totally different game from when [jujutsu] was dominating it," Frank Shamrock says. "The NHB guys are throwing punches, kicks, knees and elbows, and they understand the ground game. Unfortunately, jujutsu as a fighting style is not complete. It's a nice sport, but it's not a complete fighting style."

THE NATURAL
Favorite Fighting and Training Strategies of UFC Legend Randy Couture

by J. Michael Plott • Photos by Rick Hustead • November 2003

*R*andy "The Natural" Couture began his mixed-martial arts career six years ago by submitting Tony Halme and defeating Steven Graham to win the four-man tournament at the Ultimate Fighting Championship XIII. Five months later, he bested Vitor Belfort at UFC XV. Two months after that, he won a majority decision over Maurice Smith at the Ultimate Japan I and became the undisputed UFC heavyweight champ. Black Belt inducted him into its Hall of Fame as the 1997 Full-Contact Fighter of the Year.

Because of a contract dispute with UFC-owner Zuffa, Couture never defended his heavyweight title, and it was eventually vacated. Then on November 17, 2000, at UFC 28, he returned with a vengeance and defeated Kevin Randleman four minutes, 13 seconds into the third round. The UFC heavyweight belt had come back to papa.

He defended his title at UFC 31, defeating Pedro Rizzo with a controversial five-round decision. Couture beat him again in a rematch held at UFC 34, and this time he left no question about who was the better fighter: He took Rizzo down and pounded him until the ref stopped the bout in the third round.

At UFC 36, Couture lost to Josh Barnett, but in a twist of fate, Barnett tested positive for a banned substance and was stripped of the title. In late September 2002 at UFC 39, a series of strikes forced Couture to verbally submit to Ricco Rodriguez, causing many fans to wonder if the 39-year-old's career was over.

At the much-anticipated UFC 43, Couture, now weighing 205 pounds and debuting as a light-heavyweight, easily won the interim UFC belt by knocking out top-rated and heavily favored Chuck "The Iceman" Liddell. He became the first person in history to have held UFC belts in two weight classes.

Black Belt recently caught up with the champ while he trained for his upcoming UFC 44 bout, scheduled for September 26, 2003, in Las Vegas. As he prepared to face Tito Ortiz for the undisputed light-heavyweight title, he set aside some time to share his insights on fighting and training.

—JMP

Black Belt: You started as a wrestling champion, and now you're a mixed-martial arts champion. How have you altered your fighting strategies to cope with the differences between those two sports?

133

Randy Couture: Both are a form of kinetic chess, and the physical training for each is similar. But wrestling is more specific because you are limited in what you can do. MMA, because of all the allowed techniques and possibilities, is more difficult to prepare for.

BB: What is your overall MMA fighting strategy?

Couture: It varies from opponent to opponent because each person brings something different to a fight. Fortunately, at this level of competi-

tion, most guys you meet have fought before, and you can get tape on them. You can see them in four or five different fights and find out who they are and what they bring to a fight.

BB: So you study your opponents.

Couture: Definitely. I had to—especially when I started MMA competition as a wrestler who had never been punched and never seen a *jujutsu* stylist lying comfortably on his back waiting to nail you with a submission. I had to see what the game was and how the fighters played. For instance, when I fought Vitor Belfort, I found I was going to be fighting a guy who never had a fight last over two minutes because his hands were so fast. I knew I was going to have to survive that problem and turn the situation around so I could bring my wrestling skills into play.

BB: If you study your opponents, it stands to reason that you use a different strategy for each one.

Couture: Yes. An example would be my fights with Pedro Rizzo. Pedro is an excellent counterfighter. He waits for you to create an opening, then leaps into it. When I first fought him, I made the mistake of being too aggressive and giving him a lot of openings. He scored with leg kicks and punches because of my aggression. The next time we fought, I was much more cautious in my attacks, which largely confounded his counterfighting style. The physical conditioning and style of the opponent figure into the strategy. For instance, Chuck Liddell is a more laid-back fighter and was easier to prepare for than Tito Ortiz because Tito is very aggressive and will come out fast and hard right from the beginning. He will keep an intense pressure on for the entire fight, and I have to prepare differently for him than I did for Chuck.

BB: Has your strategy changed over the years?

Couture: Not really, but it has come into focus. I didn't really study my opponents in high school, but in college, we studied a lot of tapes of our own fights. We would try to figure out our problems and weaknesses and make corrections in our training. When I got to the world championships and Olympic level of [wrestling] competition, I was introduced to focusing on the opponent, as well. You never knew who you might be matched against, so you were always studying tapes of all the wrestlers as well as conducting scouting trips and even taking notes at competitions. You want to know things like, Does he use a right- or left-leg lead? The same thing applies to MMA fighting. You want to know if he fights southpaw, what his best technique is, how he handles this or that. Everyone has strengths and everyone uses his strengths, so when you find what they do well, you can count on them using it against you. So you prepare yourself to execute your style accordingly. You want to be able to defend against their strengths and exploit their weaknesses.

BB: For you, what is the most important factor in the ring?

Couture: Confidence. Being in a positive frame of mind and knowing what you can do and believing you can do it. You see it over and over—a guy who is tougher than hell in a gym or training environment but who freezes up or is hesitant in a real fight. That faltering is all about confidence and mental preparedness. You can get some of that preparedness from training hard and having good partners. Some of it comes from talking to yourself and practicing positive thinking. I use visualization techniques, which I used without knowing what I was doing in high school. When I got to the Olympic level, I had a team-sports psychologist who defined what I was doing naturally. Learning what I was doing instinctively helped me expand my ability to prepare mentally.

BB: Overall, how important is the mental factor?

Couture: It is crucial. It is what gets you through. When you start fighting, you are either in a winning mind-set or you are not. If you are not, you will lose. Something unexpected, like being hit hard when you didn't think it could happen, can break your focus. The way to prepare for the unexpected is to use a key word or phrase that you have prepared, one that re-centers your mind into a winning mind-set. It should be a word or phrase that brings your way of thinking back to visualizing yourself as enduring and winning the fight. That is another mental technique I picked up from my Olympic wrestling. The Russians used these techniques for years and kept them a state secret, but almost everyone at the Olympic level is now using them successfully.

BB: Do you wage mental warfare against your opponents?

Couture: No, I don't get too much into psyching out my opponents. I have noticed that because I am just myself, easygoing and quiet, I seem to freak out some of my opponents as much as if I was talking trash and trying to intimidate them.

BB: Have any opponents tried to psych you out?

Couture: Certainly. The first one was Maurice Smith, who seems to be a master of mental games. I saw him doing that to Mark Coleman when they fought. He was saying things he knew would get under Mark's skin and get him to react a certain way. Maurice couldn't do that to me. I got the impression that he wanted to play mental games with me but wasn't sure how to do it. Tito is another fighter who uses mental intimidation, saying things like, "You're going to get a beating." Actually, when I see a fighter doing that, I recognize it and tend to laugh. It's probably not the reaction they are going for.

BB: What have you found to be the optimal ratio of mental training to physical training?

Couture: The saying is that a fight is 90-percent mental and 10-percent physical, yet most fighters train 90-percent physical and 10-percent mental. That is going to have to change as MMA continues to evolve, or those fighters will be left behind. The correct ratio may be something like 60 to 40. To consistently win fights, you need a lot of mental training—more than most people do. One pitfall is to waste time thinking about things that are out of your control. I used to have that problem until I trained with the Olympic sports psychologist. Now I focus exclusively on things I can control. This type of mental training figures into every aspect of life and can help everyone attain any type of goal. Controlling negative thoughts, using positive visualization—these things help with everything from learning a new math lesson to selling more insurance to winning a street fight. Everyone should know and practice these things, no matter who you are and what your goals may be.

BB: How has aging figured into your fighting strategy? Are you doing anything differently at age 39 than you were at age 25?

Couture: I haven't noticed too many effects from aging yet. I don't think I have slowed down any, though I do take longer to recover. One thing I do differently is train smarter. I have eliminated frivolous training and use that time to focus on more relevant training. I used to do a lot of long-distance running. I have cut that down and am focusing more on sprinting [for] cardio training. I used to lift weights five to six times a week, but I have found that I don't need to be much stronger. I do need to be more tactically and technically proficient, so I have trimmed my weightlifting down to two or three times a week and substituted focus-mitt training and sparring. Basically I have become more specific in my training, which is another lesson that applies to life in general. Think honestly about your goals, whatever they may be, and prepare yourself to reach them without wasting a lot of time. Time is the one resource people never have enough of.

THE DEMANDS OF COMBAT
by Mark Hatmaker • March 2004

> *"To be a good grappler, one doesn't need size, strength, speed or extreme flexibility. One needs endurance, great technique and a certain amount of pain tolerance."*
>
> —*Gene LeBell*

Turn that quote over in your mind. Ponder it. When it comes to what it takes to make a great grappler, Gene LeBell knows what he's talking about. His observation isn't far off for the striking arts, either. As a matter of fact, I would say his words should be taken to heart by all combat athletes.

Now don't get me wrong: Size is great. Strength is great. Speed is a conditioned blessing. What we must glean from LeBell's quote is the importance of endurance and conditioning in this game. We must also

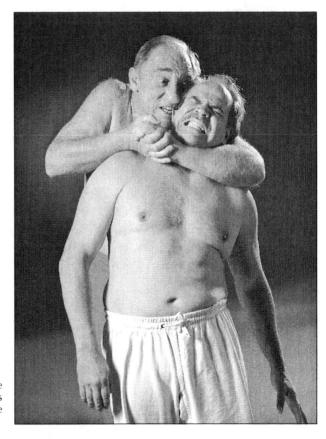

Grappling legend Gene LeBell demonstrates his impeccable technique on the hapless Armando Guerrero.

remember the saying heard in any boxing gym worth its salt: Fights are won in the gym, not in the ring.

Why am I pushing the importance of conditioning? Because I want you to focus your goals toward your specific athletic endeavor and stop hamstringing yourself with conditioning methodologies and practices related to other sports. I want you to get off the supplement kick and invest your hard-earned time and money in the sweat equity of hard-core somatotrophic conditioning. The ideal would be to find your natural weight and play to its strengths, rather than continually striving to be something other than the heavyweight, middleweight, lightweight or flyweight you are. Toughness is found in the character and performance of the athlete, not in the measuring tape or scale readout.

Although I happen to agree with LeBell's quote, it's not to say that size and strength don't matter. They do. That's why we have weight classes. We lean toward his advice because of time considerations, genetics and the law of averages.

Right now, I weigh 175 pounds, so it's pretty safe to say there are bigger and stronger people out there. I can pump iron until all hours of the night and consume all the supplements my bank account can sustain, but my strength and size gains will never match the naturally fit fighter of 225 pounds. The time and money lost trying to beat my genetic predisposition—let alone my attempts at maintaining this artificial state—would violate the laws of economy and effectiveness. I would be better off ignoring size increases and investing my time in modest strength gains while developing endurance and technique to truly better my odds of success in my sport.

So are strength and size important? Yes, but you must develop what you have and not ignore the true goal of your chosen sport to chase powerlifting goals—unless powerlifting is your sport. Concentrate on modest strength gains and exercises that will develop muscular endurance. By doing so, your strength will increase appreciably to keep you competitive within your weight class.

One last thought: You can build what LeBell calls a "certain amount of pain tolerance" by developing your ability to perform each exercise as one continuous set. Ideally, the calisthenics should be executed with no breaks during each exercise or between different exercises. In other words, there are no sets—just crank it until you're done. There are no breaks in a fight, so avoid them in training. The degree of mental toughness that is tempered by this do-or-die approach will serve you well in competition.

THE JUJUTSU EFFECT
The Grappling Art Catapults B.J. Penn to the Top of the UFC Welterweight Division

Interview by Edward Pollard • Photos by Sara Fogan • June 2004

*D*espite having an impressive mixed-martial arts record (now 7-1-1) built on a solid striking foundation, B.J. "The Prodigy" Penn had been unable to secure the Ultimate Fighting Championship's lightweight title. The one-time jujutsu world champion was beginning to inhabit that limbo where potential never quite matures into success. To all but his closest associates, he appeared reckless and desperate when word spread that he would face Matt Hughes for the welterweight title at the UFC 46. Hughes had ruled that class for more than two years, dominating every challenger and seeming invincible. Nevertheless, Penn defied the odds and won the bout decisively. Now the world is looking at him with different eyes. Black Belt recently spoke with the new champ about his training and fighting methods and about the shifting pathways of fortune.

—E.P.

Black Belt: How did you prepare for your bout with Matt Hughes at the UFC 46?

B.J. Penn: I trained very hard for the fight, but never did I go past the point that I wasn't excited about it—where I'd say, "Hey, man, I'm bored

Penn's background in Brazilian jujutsu has given him an arsenal of grappling techniques that target all parts of an opponent's body.

141

of training." I just kept myself real happy and trained just enough to stay right on that line. I always had a great mental focus for the fight.

BB: How do you determine when you're overtraining?

Penn: When you don't want to go and you're not having fun. This is what I love to do, [so] how can I not be having fun? [If that happens,] it's because I'm doing it too much. You've got to have a balance—a *yin* and *yang* kind of thing, I guess.

BB: What happened when you overtrained in the past?

Penn: I wasn't really interested or motivated. Because I used to go so hard for months before the fight, by the time I got to the fight, I didn't want to do anything.

BB: You pretty much fought the match during training.

Penn: Exactly.

BB: Can you describe any of the techniques or strategies you utilize in the octagon?

Penn: I always do a lot of wrestling, *jujutsu,* boxing and kickboxing. I just go in there and try to beat the guy however I can.

BB: Your bout with Hughes was amazing because it looked like he didn't really have the time or space to do anything.

Penn: I think he's never been on the ground with a jujutsu world champion before. There's a big difference.

BB: Was there a favorite move that you used during that match?

Penn: No, I like all the moves. I really don't have a favorite. Everything changes for me. I might like a move for two weeks and then, boom, I'm not doing that move anymore. Even if I feel like it, I just don't do it anymore and I [go on to] different things. The game is constantly evolving within me.

BB: Let's say someone reading this interview wants to fight like you do. What advice would you give?

Penn: Keep yourself open, learn new techniques and always try stuff. Sometimes you're going to get in bad positions—you've got to learn how it feels to be winning and losing and tired and everything.

BB: How do you deal with fatigue?

Penn: During the fight, you realize that you're always going to get tired, but you've just got to fight through it and keep going. Your body's always going to get to that one point where it's not feeling great, but that's when you've got to be mentally strong and just keep going, even though your muscles are getting tired. I think it comes with experience.

BB: Did you have a particular strategy for the Hughes fight?

Penn: I was going to try to knock him out standing up, then move it to

B.J. Penn (top) kneels beside his opponent (1). To execute the technique, he repositions his left hand on the man's lapel (2). Next, Penn shifts his pelvis over his opponent's head, breaking the man's grip on his pants (3). Because he has maintained his hold on the lapel, Penn need only extend his right arm behind the opponent's neck and grab his uniform to complete the choke (4).

the ground and try to submit him. I wasn't going to let him take me down. If [I'd been] put on my back, I had a million moves ready to go. I really trained in jujutsu hard for this fight. I was doing all kinds of different guard work—like what might happen when I'm up against the fence. I was going to let him feel the pressure right away, let him know that I'm here and that with every punch I'm going to try to knock him out. I wanted to make him feel pressure the whole time no matter what happened. He [was] going to feel me coming after him, trying to beat him.

BB: How did you feel in the days and hours leading up to the match?

Penn: I felt great, happy. I knew this was one fight that I could possibly get hurt in—like a cut or something—but I knew I had way more skill than he did. I knew I was just as strong as he was. Everybody was acting like he was a lot stronger than me, but [I think] I'm one of the strongest people for that weight.

BB: Did you feel at any point that you were in danger of losing control of the action?

Penn: No, but only because I made sure of that. I made sure not to even let him get a chance to reverse me. I knew once I got on top of him, it was going to be really hard for him to get me off.

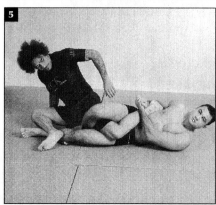

When forced to fend off a standing opponent, UFC welterweight champ Penn maneuvers his body to trap the man's left leg (1). Penn uses his legs to topple his foe (2-3), then key-locks his right leg around the man's left leg (4). He completes the heel hook by applying lateral pressure with both arms and his torso (5).

BB: For you, where did the journey to the top begin?

Penn: We were always boxing in my front yard. This *taekwondo* teacher moved down the street from my house and gave me some jujutsu lessons. He kept bothering my dad, [who] was like, "Please go down once so this guy leaves me alone."

BB: Did you learn any taekwondo from him?

Penn: No, I never did TKD. The TKD teacher did a couple classes of jujutsu. He lived on my street, and he would see all the kids come to my house and box. He wanted some jujutsu partners to work out with. We never did jujutsu or anything, and he would tell my dad to have us kids come and roll around with him. I was like: "No, no, there's no need to. What a waste of my time, I'm already the toughest guy in the world." I was probably 16 or 17 when I [finally] went down there, and the guy choked me out and armbarred me, and then I moved from there. I thought if I could do this, I could beat up the whole town. That's how I started.

BB: Hawaiian culture and the people in general are perceived as happy and laid back. That doesn't exactly fit with the image most people have of champion fighters.

Penn: Everybody over here fights and is into boxing and kickboxing. Even around here, people know about grappling. Hawaii's big for the mixed martial arts. All the kids wrestle at home and in their backyard all the time.

BB: What are your plans for the future? Will you continue to compete in the welterweight division?

Penn: I'm just picking single fights for now, whether lightweight or above. I'm going to look for the biggest and best fights. I'm not going to fight all the up-and-comers trying to make a name. It's time to fight all the best guys, so that's what I'm going to do.

CHUCK LIDDELL
The UFC's Heavy Hitter Weighs in on His Favorite Ranges, Techniques and Strategies for Winning

Interview by Robert W. Young • Photos by Rick Hustead • August 2004

*I*n the minds of many traditionalists, the mixed-martial arts genre has produced two standout stars: Maurice Smith, the kickboxer who knocked out Brazilian-jujutsu expert Marcus "Conan" Silveira with a couple of kicks to the noggin, and Chuck Liddell, the karate and kempo stylist who has stood toe-to-toe with the MMA world's toughest fighters and dropped the majority of them with kicks and punches that could have been drawn from the arsenal of any traditional practitioner. In this exclusive Black Belt interview, Liddell, fresh from his light-heavyweight victory over Tito Ortiz in the Ultimate Fighting Championship 47, talks about the lessons he's learned from his years in the striking arts, as well as the best ways you can avoid reinventing the wheel and learn the lessons of the Chuck Liddell School of Hard Knocks.

—Editor

Black Belt: What's your martial arts background? Everyone knows you trained in kempo. Was it your first art?

Chuck Liddell: The first was *koei-kan* karate, which I started when I was 12. When I went to school, I was still doing that at the martial arts club. I went to kempo in 1993. And I've been wrestling since I was 14.

BB: What did karate, kempo and wrestling bring to your mixed-martial arts skill set?

Liddell: Wrestling gave me better balance, mobility and positioning. Karate gave me a strong background in striking. Kempo gave me my hands and my kicks. I've always had hard kicks—even when I started kickboxing, I was 20-2 with 16 knockouts, eight of which were by kicks.

BB: In the ring, do you favor high kicks or low kicks?

Liddell: I like to mix them up. And I've always liked to throw head kicks. They work, and they're definitely a crowd pleaser.

BB: What skills did you *not* learn from the traditional arts that you later determined were essential in the MMA ring?

Liddell: I found I was limited in techniques for the ground. I knew I needed more, so I started Brazilian *jujutsu* with John Lewis, a Las Vegas-based trainer who used to study with Gene LeBell.

BB: Did you train with any other big-name grapplers?

Liddell: I did a class with Bas Rutten and Marco Ruas—I did a lot of things when I was starting out. I was smart enough to know that I needed to learn [ground] skills—or at least how to stay out of them.

BB: What makes Brazilian jujutsu so indispensable for MMA fighters?

Liddell: If you don't know it, sooner or later you'll get caught.

BB: You used to work as a bartender and a bouncer, and now you're an MMA champion. How close is what you do in the octagon to real self-defense in a club?

Liddell: MMA is the safest way you can practice your skills without getting in a real fight. It's the best way to simulate using techniques that could inflict permanent damage in a less controlled environment.

BB: Some fighters like to charge in and go for their favorite move. Others like to wait for their opponent to leave an opening they can exploit. What about you? Do you have an overall fight strategy?

Liddell: Everybody has a game plan going into a fight—what things you want to do and what you think you can do.

BB: Does the plan stay the same from opponent to opponent?

Liddell: It depends on the person you're fighting. They all have similarities, but you have to match your style against his. Against a guy who's not so good, I'll counterfight. Other guys are hard to stop if you do it that way.

Although he isn't crazy about knee thrusts, Chuck Liddell (left) recognizes their usefulness in the clinch.

The overhand right: Chuck Liddell (right) faces Tony Diaz (1). When the time is right, Liddell uncorks the punch (2), which travels above the opponent's guard and lands on his jaw (3).

BB: How do you deal with a long-range fighter, one who likes to stay on the outside and use kicks when the gap is being closed?

Liddell: I deal with that [situation] well. I like being at a distance. It gives me more time to strike and more time to react. In wrestling, you learn not to shoot unless you can touch your opponent. So when you're out of his range, there's not as much he can do to you.

BB: So you stay back and throw a kick when he starts coming in?

Liddell: Not necessarily. I like to stay on the end of my punches. If you watch my last fight with Tito [Ortiz], one of the things I didn't do is what a lot of people do: They get his back to the cage where he's covering, then choke themselves up and get too close. Then he body-locks them and takes them down. But I stayed far enough away to stay at the end of my punches.

BB: What techniques do you prefer to use in that range?

Liddell: I like to mix them all together. I watched Roy Jones Jr. a while ago talking about combinations. He said he'll throw 15 or 20 punches, and his opponent has to try to block all of them because he doesn't know which one is going to be the powerful one.

BB: Are you a believer in the big four punches: the jab, cross, hook and uppercut?

Liddell: Yeah, basically. That's boxing. But there are some extra ones, too. The overhand right is good to use every once in a while because you can catch people with it.

BB: Do any other traditional martial arts strikes get used in the octagon?

Liddell: You see the hammerfist a lot and some spinning punches and kicks.

BB: Speaking of kicks, which ones do you find best-suited for use in MMA competition?

Liddell: I like the roundhouse to the head ... and the leg kick and whip kick.

BB: What do you mean by whip kick?

Liddell: It snaps. I usually make it look like a roundhouse is coming down to his leg, then I change directions and put it up to his head—boom.

BB: How do you deal with a kicker?

Liddell: Grab him.

BB: Move in and grab him?

Liddell: Stand and grab him.

BB: So even with your background in the striking arts, you would never try to out-kick a kicker? You would always try to do something he's not doing?

Liddell: It depends on who he is. If he has no ground and I do, then I'll [take him down]. Even if I know I'm a better striker than he is, if I know I'm a lot better on the ground, why stand up and smack? One punch can change the fight.

BB: What about in the middle range? What do you generally do there?

Liddell: I like elbows. When you land a clean one, it's a hard shot. The only thing I don't like about using them is you can cut your opponent really deep, and that can mean the fight gets stopped for the wrong reason. Knees I throw pretty much to the body, but I've never been a big kneer. Because I like to try to keep my space, I do a lot of circling and pivoting.

BB: Once you and your opponent hit the mat, what's your goal? Submission techniques, punches...?

Liddell: Mostly striking. Don't get me wrong: If the other guy gives it to

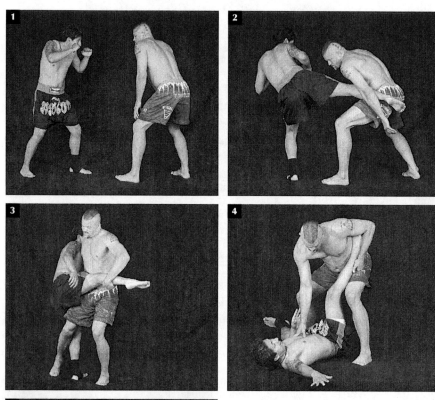

Kick catch with ground and pound: The opponent (left) sizes up Chuck Liddell (1), then unleashes a low roundhouse, which Liddell traps (2). The mixed-martial arts champ scoots forward (3) and sweeps the opponent to the ground (4). He then drops and begins a barrage of strikes (5).

me, I'll take a submission. But I'm not going to go out of my way to force it, and I'm not going to risk being in a [bad] position to force it. Remember that to get position on the ground, you need technique. It doesn't matter where you start hitting—you'll end up being in the dominant position. I'm looking to get my opponent in a dominant position where I can pound on him better and hurt him.

BB: When it comes to finishing techniques, which do you favor?

Liddell: I like chokes and armbars mainly; I always have. One thing about leg locks I don't like is that my legs are going to be as exposed as yours, basically. You have as good a shot at finishing me as I have at finishing you. Another thing is, if you're not careful with them in training, it's easy to get hurt. If you don't understand them, [a lock will feel uncomfortable] and then pop in no time at all. A big challenge is how to make sparring as realistic as possible without getting hurt all the time. It's a juggling act.

BB: Are there any parts of the traditional martial arts that you just have no use for in competition—either because the rules don't allow them or because they don't work? For instance, some people say judo is a great art for the ground but in an MMA match, the throwing doesn't work the way it does in a judo match.

Liddell: Those throws do work, but you've got to get your opponent to push on you more. And when you don't have his *gi* to grab, it's really hard to force a throw.

BB: When you're out there striking, are you looking just to unload on your opponent—no matter where you hit him, it's OK—or are you looking to hit a precise target?

Liddell: I don't really shoot for precise targets; I shoot for bigger targets. With punches, I like to aim for the chin. With kicks, I like to go for the legs. Against a wrestler, I'll go for the high stuff, too. I always want to try to hurt the guy.

Tech Tips From The Iceman

Kneebar from the top: Despite his penchant for ground striking, Chuck Liddell believes the kneebar is an effective finishing technique that can be executed from the half-guard whether you're on the top or bottom. The key is setting up your opponent and catching him by surprise. If he's lying on his back and you're in his half-guard straddling his right leg, begin by redirecting his attention toward his upper body by appearing to attack his arms. As soon as he's distracted, slip your outside (left) knee across his abdomen and lift his left knee. Next, continue your motion across his body and fall to his left side while using your arms to pin the leg against your chest. As you arch your back, your hips exert pressure against his knee and your right leg keeps him from maneuvering to relieve it.

Kneebar from the bottom: When you're on your back with your opponent in your half-guard, your first priority is to break his balance and roll him to one side, Liddell says. As he kneels over you on your left side, turn so you're facing him. Slip your right arm under his armpit and your left arm behind his right knee. Press your left calf into the back of his left knee and your right shin into his stomach. Next, use your right arm to push him and your right leg to lift him as you rotate his body counterclockwise away from your head. Immediately hook your left leg over his butt while pinning his right knee against your chest, then execute the kneebar by arching your back to apply pressure against the joint.

Heel hook from the bottom: It's possible to perform a heel hook when your opponent is mounted on top of you, but first you must get out of the mount, Liddell says. Place your hands on his lower abdomen and your forearms on his thighs, then thrust your hips upward and push his body to your right. At the same time, turn toward him (to your right) and place your right leg between his legs as you use your right arm to push his upper body away. Next, throw your left leg across his right thigh and arch your

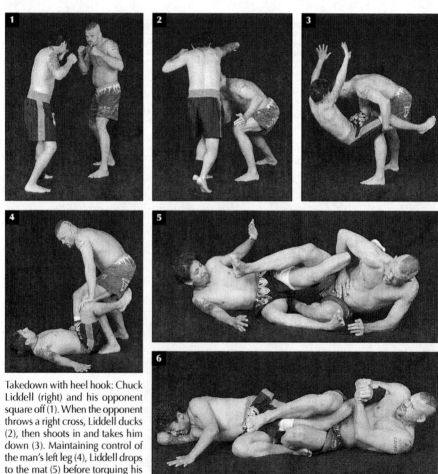

Takedown with heel hook: Chuck Liddell (right) and his opponent square off (1). When the opponent throws a right cross, Liddell ducks (2), then shoots in and takes him down (3). Maintaining control of the man's left leg (4), Liddell drops to the mat (5) before torquing his heel for a submission (6).

back to get your butt as close as possible to his while you trap his right foot under your left arm. To finish him, reach back with your left hand and scoop his trapped heel with your forearm. Lock your hands for added power and twist your torso clockwise to apply pressure to his heel.

Heel hook from the half-guard: You can also employ the heel hook while lying on your back holding your opponent in your half-guard. Start by placing your right shin against his stomach and controlling his right leg with your left arm. Then use your right arm and leg to shove his upper body away from your head. If he cooperates, execute a kneebar from the bottom as described above. If he changes his direction and starts to sit back, Liddell says, hook his foot under your left armpit and use your forearm to apply lateral pressure to his heel.

WARRIOR YOGA
Frank Shamrock Harnesses the Power of the Ancient Art for Modern No-Holds-Barred Competition

by Drew Archer and Edward Pollard • Photos courtesy of Frank Shamrock • October 2004

The traditional martial arts have always focused on training the body, mind and spirit, and they've served practitioners well for thousands of years. However, during the past decade, a new method has emerged. It's an innovative approach built on the freedom to learn from all styles without regard for why a particular skill was created or where it originated. It's been dubbed the "mixed martial arts."

Like traditional martial artists, MMA enthusiasts focus on physical training and conditioning. By subjecting their bodies to unfamiliar demands, they transform themselves into some of the most well-rounded athletes in the world. Heavy-duty cardio workouts, weightlifting sessions and sparring matches all play an important role in their daily routines.

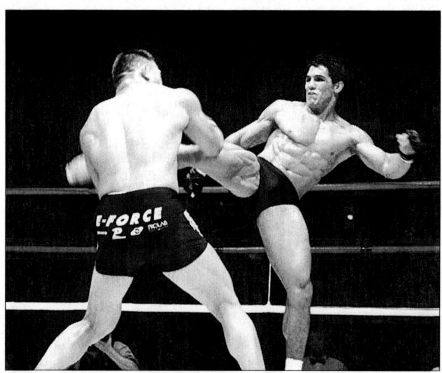

Frank Shamrock smashes Enson Inoue with a body kick at the Japan Vale Tudo in 1997.

Jeremy Corbell created Warrior Yoga, then helped Frank Shamrock adapt its teachings to no-holds-barred training.

Because they constantly test their skills in the ring, they're always in need of more efficient ways to respond to the stresses they face. They already know it pays to study a variety of fighting disciplines and blend the best techniques into a cohesive whole. That has made the technical side of the martial arts grow by leaps and bounds during the past 10 years.

Unfortunately, many of these athletes have been so focused on developing their physique that they've neglected the mental and spiritual aspects of the traditional arts. They're just starting to discover that competition challenges the brain as much as the body. They're learning that having a mechanism to cope with the mental ups and downs of limited-rules combat is vital to success. For a few of them, that mechanism is a modern interpretation of a centuries-old discipline from India: yoga.

Connecting

Frank Shamrock, one of the premier MMA fighters in the world, long ago recognized the value of incorporating yoga into a holistic approach to the mixed martial arts. Renowned for using cross-training to kick, punch and grapple his way to the top of the food chain, he relied on yoga to keep his mind and body in optimal shape. Before a bout, he would use it to prepare mentally and physically, and afterward he would use it to heal

The deep breathing methods taught in Warrior Yoga can help mixed martial artists maintain their energy levels in competition.

any injuries he sustained.

Soon after discovering the value of yoga, Shamrock ran into Jeremy Corbell, creator of an entity known as Warrior Yoga. He immediately knew he'd found someone who could understand what he needed in terms of training, healing and sustaining his energy levels despite constant pressure from within and without. In many ways, the two had been operating on parallel tracks, and each offered the other the experience and wisdom he'd gleaned from his chosen field.

"Warrior Yoga is his program, his philosophy," Shamrock says. "My experience is in training. I did a lot of similar techniques in stretching and working out, so when we started to train together, there was a lot of the same thing going on. He had targeted areas of the body and developed a mentor approach that I'd had for fighting, but not for general conditioning or life."

Once he delved into Warrior Yoga, Shamrock noticed he was getting injured less often because his body was more balanced and toned, he says. He also identified two other areas in which big improvements were made: stretching and meditation.

Stretching

Early in his career, Shamrock learned that stretching should be a major component of all serious training programs, but even as MMA competition rose to prominence, many athletes considered it taboo. Nevertheless, he adjusted his training accordingly, and he still enjoys the benefits of regularly elongating his muscles, which can boost strength and explosive power.

"I use the stretching portion of Warrior Yoga for general conditioning and balance training, as well as for breathing and relaxing," he says. "I like to go through 10 basic postures—most are on the mat but a couple are standing. I like to go through the range of flexion. I think of yoga as a slowed-down version of a mat drill or *kata.*"

The physical side of yoga practice benefits martial arts training because it's conditioning-oriented and balance-oriented, he says. "Striking is very aerobic; you maximize your body in the upright position, which is cardiovascular. Your center of balance and speed give you distance and the ability to do damage. Yoga is nice because it reinforces your balance. For grappling, you need conditioning and technique, and yoga goes right to the source of conditioning."

Shamrock likes to complete a yoga workout before and after training, sparring, wrestling and teaching. "I use it to heat up—to stress or warm

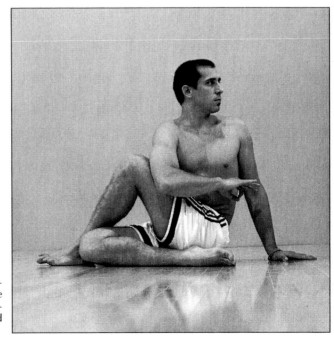

One benefit of yoga practice is the elongation the muscles undergo as various postures are assumed and held.

In Warrior Yoga sessions, meditation helps students work through the pain they feel and actually use it to gauge their progress.

up certain areas of my body—and reinforce the techniques physically," he says. "I usually take 10 or 15 minutes before any really strenuous workout and do a calming, stretching, energizing yoga workout. When I do it, I keep in mind the technique, concept or theory I'm going to train."

Meditation

Yoga practice is designed to take students to the edge of their physical capacity. They quickly find that holding the poses for any length of time reveals the limitations of their flexibility, thus helping them learn how to recognize pain as a marker and not simply a warning. For fighters, meditation and focused breathing are the keys to tolerating the burning sensation that accompanies the stretch.

Pain management becomes crucial because every serious yoga student courts this edge of performance to measure his progress. Shamrock is keenly aware of what happens at that edge and uses meditation to still his mind when he gets there. "I start with the breath and lengthen it out a bit," he says. "Whatever I'm thinking of, I breathe it away. Whatever is there, I say, 'OK, that's really not necessary,' and exhale it with my breath."

Obviously, deep breathing is an integral part of yoga meditation. In a prolonged battle, remembering to breathe properly can be challenging. Normal or shallow breathing is reflexive, but focused breathing doesn't come naturally. It must be learned.

For Shamrock, a typical meditation/breathing session lasts from five minutes to 10 minutes and involves soft lighting, music and a peaceful environment. During that time, he strives to achieve a higher level of awareness by emptying his mind—by warming up his brain to do nothing, he says. In everyday terms, it involves reducing the amount of attention paid to distracting thoughts, especially those that arise in response to the pain induced by stretching.

When Shamrock is ready to go deep into a meditative state, he often combines a form of self-hypnosis with a long walk, thus lowering his energy output. Gradually he adds layers of intent back into his consciousness until he's ready to begin acting physically again. It's the ultimate preparation for the ultimate sport.

Potential

The Shamrock-Corbell partnership has given rise to a new level of understanding in the mixed martial arts. By sharing information about the worlds of athletic and holistic training, they've resurrected the true design and purpose of fighting arts that were created millennia ago: the melding of the body, mind and spirit. The martial arts community is better off because of it.

Yoga enhances flexibility while it conditions the muscles and joints.

WANNA BE THE ULTIMATE FIGHTER?
Randy Couture and Chuck Liddell Will Take You to the Top—Just Like They're Doing on Their New Reality-TV Show!

by J. Michael Plott, Robert W. Young and Edward Pollard • March 2005

"**A**s real as it gets" is often used as the tag line for the Ultimate Fighting Championship, because the event's bouts are as close to a real fight as the law and the fighters' safety permit.

Starting in January 2005, that catchphrase will also refer to Spike TV's newest reality show, *The Ultimate Fighter.* It stars current UFC light-heavyweight champ Randy Couture and No. 1 light-heavyweight contender Chuck Liddell as the team captains.

In the program, 16 aspiring mixed martial artists will meet one another, then train for three grueling days under the watchful eyes of Couture and Liddell. After the testing period, the captains will take turns picking fighters to form their teams.

The two groups will then begin training under their respective leaders, and the fighters will meet each other in real MMA fights every week, with the loser leaving the show. The final episode will be a two-hour live event featuring a middleweight and light-heavyweight bout between the four surviving fighters to determine which team prevails. The two victors will be seeded into a future UFC.

Following the formula of other reality shows, *The Ultimate Fighter* will have periodic physical challenges for the contestants. The winners will receive a prize, such as being able to select the next matchup between the teams.

All 16 athletes will live in a huge Las Vegas home, which they won't be allowed to leave except to train. They'll have virtually no contact with the outside world: no television, radio, phone or newspapers. A battery of cameras will record all the interactions that fill the gaps between bouts and workouts.

Although none of the 16 fighters is a pro, each has amateur MMA experience and dreams of a career in the budding sport. They were recruited after invitations were shown at the end of UFC broadcasts and mailed to smaller MMA organizations, said UFC President Dana White.

Several hundred applications poured in from excellent prospects. A few, however, came from people who were somewhat less qualified. "We have videos from people who have no experience in fighting or even martial arts," White said. "Guys who say they've trained themselves from books, videos and street fights sent videos of themselves in the basement breaking boards or demonstrating their moves on training dummies.

"One of my favorites is a guy who says he's a pool-hustling fighter who challenges bar patrons to play pool. If they lose, they have to fight him. He says he's currently undefeated, though I'm not sure if he's talking about playing pool or fighting."

White, who's not a fan of reality television, made it his mission to ensure that *The Ultimate Fighter* would be several notches above the standard fare. "I tuned in to one episode of *The Contender* because I'm a longtime boxing fan and wanted to see a match," he said. "I suffered through most of a very boring hour just to see the match and came away vastly disappointed. The actual boxing portion of the show was short and obviously

Photo by Rick Hustead

In *The Ultimate Fighter*, a team of martial artists coached by Randy Couture (left) will face off against a team coached by Chuck Liddell.

cut. At the conclusion when they interviewed the fighters, both looked just fine. Any martial artist knows you can't trade full-contact techniques without some trace of injury unless both fighters are taking it pretty easy on each other.

"In our show, just during the initial three-day training/testing period, our guys had sprains, bruises and even stitches—all before they were even chosen for a team. They really want to win, and they bang hard. These are real fights, and we show all of it."

COUTURE'S CRASH COURSE
Interview by Robert W. Young

Black Belt: How do you start training someone who's new to the mixed martial arts?

Randy Couture: The first thing you need to find out is if he has a background in wrestling or judo or some other combative sport. You can play off that and develop other skills. The person's basic fitness level is also important. You have to teach the kind of fitness needed for MMA competition through cardiovascular training, anaerobic training and inner-strength training.

Photo by J. Michael Plott

Aspiring champions work out on the set of Spike TV's *The Ultimate Fighter*.

One of Couture's favorite strikes is the reinforced elbow to the head.

Photo by Rick Hustead

BB: What kind of athletic background besides combat sports would be an advantage? Football, sprinting, long-distance running?

Couture: All those sports bring a particular foundation, at least at a fitness level, that you can play off, but I'm not sure any of them offers a distinct advantage in MMA. However, it's important that the person has competed in something and has a competitive spirit.

BB: Is competitive spirit something a person either has or doesn't have? Or can it be taught?

Couture: You can certainly test it. There are so many innate qualities that a person either has or doesn't have, but you can still educate him, push him and see how far he can go. And you can constantly push that wall back until he can go further and further. Most people can go a lot further than they think.

BB: Once you evaluate the person and learn about his background, where do you go from there?

Couture: Being at the top level in this sport, I've developed some tools and techniques for conditioning a fighter's body the way it needs to be conditioned and for developing the skill sets he needs to be well-rounded. So the next step is to set a training regimen that builds conditioning through sprinting, running, biking, weightlifting and circuit training. It also includes time on the mat, light sparring, mitt work, ground training and wrestling. The goal is to develop skills and tools he can rely on when he needs to.

BB: Do you agree with those martial artists who insist you can get all the strength and endurance you need from doing your art, as long as you do it enough?

Couture: To some extent that can be true. There are plenty of examples of people who don't do any of that extra stuff. But when you get to the higher levels and want to be the top dog, you have to do the extra stuff that will distinguish you from the others. You have to do those extras like increasing your foot speed and improving your dynamic, explosive power.

BB: What comes next for the budding fighter?

Couture: Light sparring and putting him in different situations. You have to ensure he has an open mind and checks his ego at the door. He has to believe that he's always going to learn something, and he has to put himself out there. He has to risk being tapped out, risk losing—not only in training but also in fights that will challenge him.

BB: Say you're training a grappler who's got some decent skills. Do you try to perfect his ability on the ground, or do you focus on striking because it's his weakness?

Couture: I would spend more time—and this is the perspective I have as a wrestler who'd never been in a striking sport—on striking. Weaknesses have to be made into strengths. But the second you neglect one area of his training, somebody will point it out to him in competition. With a grappler, I would spend a lot of time on his hands and his ability to stop takedowns.

BB: For the grappling portion of his training, which arts would you draw from?

Couture: Certainly wrestling and *jujutsu* would be big components. I've also learned some things from judo players that I've found applicable. Wrestling is great because of the mat sense and intensity it brings, as well as the ability to take opponents down and control them from the top position. Jujutsu will teach him how to be on the bottom, how to fight on his butt and back, and how to find ways to not only submit his opponent but also to sweep and change positions.

I would couple that with Greco-Roman wrestling, especially the clinch position, because in mixed martial arts, a fighter's posture is so much more upright than in most grappling sports. It applies very well for infighting and being able to take an opponent down while controlling him.

BB: What about for striking?

Couture: Western boxing and kickboxing are the most effective striking arts for this combative sport.

BB: Why not Thai boxing?

Couture: I think Thai boxing fits with what Greco-Roman and clinch fighting do best: infighting. The elbows and knees are very effective tools at close range.

BB: What are the essential skills and techniques you would cover?

Couture: The fighter needs good balance and footwork. He has to be able to defend himself, use his hands and elbows to cover his head, parry punches, and slip punches, kicks and knees. He also needs to be able to throw a proper punch and execute good combinations of kicks and knees.

From there, he should move into clinch range, where he works inside control, neck wrestling, trapping and ways to not only strike but also to take his opponent off his feet. He has to meld wrestling with striking, especially from the open position. He can't just go out with the intention of setting up his opponent and taking him down. It's too obvious to work, too easy to counter.

BB: Is that because fighters these days are too smart to fall into the traps that might have worked during the early days of the UFC?

Photo by Rick Hustead

Because of his extensive wrestling experience, Couture knows the value of control techniques on the ground.

Couture: Yeah. Everybody's cross-training, learning wrestling skills, learning to counter takedowns. A fighter's got to be prepared and understand that his opponent is going to know what's coming.

And then he's got to work at being adept on the ground—whether he's on the top or bottom. He's got to be able to scramble, sweep and get back to a neutral position—and find in those transitions opportunities to submit his opponent. Or if he gets his opponent down, he's got to be able to keep him at a disadvantage so he can chip away at him.

BB: Would you also teach him how to use the environment—the fence and the mats of the octagon?

Couture: There are definitely tactics for fighting in a ring and a cage. There are things he has to watch out for and things he can take advantage of.

BB: How do you approach strategy? Is there one you always teach, or are there four or five ways you would introduce?

Couture: It varies from opponent to opponent. Obviously, it's more difficult training younger fighters because you don't have a lot of experience with them and their capabilities, and you generally don't know much about their opponents. But as a fighter moves into the higher ranks, you get the opportunity to see a lot of tape of his opponents. You notice their

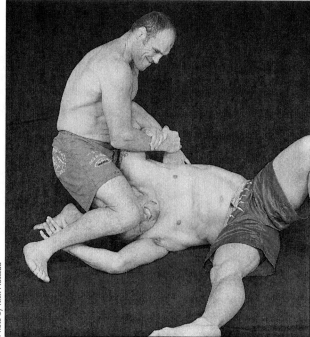

Photo by Rick Hustead

Submission techniques such as this arm lock form an essential component of the arsenal all mixed-martial artists need to know, says Couture.

THE ULTIMATE GUIDE TO MIXED MARTIAL ARTS

tendencies and how their strengths and weaknesses will match up with your fighter's strengths and weaknesses, then you figure out ways to win. They have to be willing to break themselves down and be honest about [their abilities]—and then go to the gym and do what it takes to execute that game plan.

BB: Did you encounter any special challenges while filming *The Ultimate Fighter?*

Couture: There were a lot of challenges for the athletes that created some challenges for me. Guys came in with different levels of conditioning. Some were really prepared and ready to go, and others had no idea what they were getting themselves into and consequently suffered physically, which made it difficult for me to push them.

Some guys had better skill sets in some areas versus others. If I tried to focus on their weaknesses without singling out individuals, I couldn't spend the proper amount of time with others who didn't need that extra training.

In general, I put them through a peaking phase as if, at the end of this, they were going to have a big fight. I tried to get them physically in the same kind of shape I get in for a fight.

BB: What have I left out?

Couture: The biggest piece that guys miss is the mental skill it takes not only to get through a training camp, but also to deal with the adversity of competition. They have to deal with the negative self-talk, and the jitters and the pressures of going out and performing in front of a bunch of people. They have to relax enough to do what they're trained to do.

BB: At the beginning of the UFC, it seemed like it was average guy against average guy, art against art. But now it's Superman against Superman, and everybody knows every relevant art. Seeing how much the sport has progressed, are you limited with respect to how good you can make an average person who might weigh 170 pounds and have done 10 years of karate?

Couture: It depends on the individual. We're all blessed with certain gifts and abilities, and that average guy has those things, too. Maybe he just hasn't tapped into them yet, and for some people, it's going to take longer than others. There are so many variables that play into making a good fighter; mind-set is probably the most important. What does he think his limitations are? Is he willing to do the work to get where he wants to go? It's almost more important than any physical gift he has.

BB: What's the optimal age to attend a training camp like the one shown in *The Ultimate Fighter*? If you're a champ when you're 40, that's one thing. But if you start when you're 40, that might be totally different.

Couture: Again, it depends on your background: What did you do in that 40 years? I'm 41, but I've spent my entire life since I was 10 competing in sports. To take a 40-year-old guy who's never competed in anything and get him up to speed physically and mentally for this combative sport is a big challenge, but it could be done. Will he be a world champion in a year? Probably not. Will he be able to compete within a year? He probably could.

BB: What advice would you give to people who will read this article and aspire to compete in the UFC?

Couture: The environment is a huge factor, so they should find a place where they're comfortable and where they're going to be exposed to all the pieces of the mixed-martial arts fight game. They should find a group of guys they can trust, guys who are going to teach them things and help them progress as a person and a fighter. You're only as good as your workout partners.

BB: What about advice for people who aren't quite ready to move into a training camp? What about that 16-year-old in Kansas who thinks, "When

Photo by Rick Hustead

Defending against an opponent's attack is important, but so is immediately following up with a counterattack.

THE ULTIMATE GUIDE TO MIXED MARTIAL ARTS

I'm 20, I really want to be a fighter, but now I'm living at home and training three days a week"?

Couture: It's not too early at 16; he still has to find that right place, and hopefully it'll be fairly close to home. It'll be a little more accessible when he turns 18 because he can go his own way. If he has a wrestling program in his school, that's a good place to start because it's an organized sport, and most programs are pretty good at developing at least one piece of the game.

BB: What about other options like going to the YMCA and doing boxing two days a week? Or lifting weights at home?

Couture: Those are all pieces of the puzzle. If all he can work on where he's at now is striking, then he should go to town on that and look for a different situation to add the other skills down the road.

LIDDELL'S LEADERSHIP LESSON
Interview by Edward Pollard

Black Belt: How do you take an athlete who's had some training but is still fairly inexperienced to a place where he can compete in the octagon?

Chuck Liddell: The first thing you've got to do is check where he's at, what he's good at and where his strengths lie. A lot of times, he doesn't even know. He may think his strength is in one thing when actually he's better at something else.

BB: If a guy comes to the gym and says he wants to compete, how do you assess his skill?

Liddell: Usually, I take what he says he knows and check him out on that. This is for guys who come to me and want to fight. I don't ask them to fight. You can't teach someone to want to fight. He has to like fighting.

BB: Let's say someone arrives with grappling skills and proves he knows a few things.

Liddell: If he's got good submission skills or takedowns and he's a good wrestler, that will be the thing we work on the least. We'll try to keep it sharp because that's the main part of his game, but I don't need to work with him on that too much. I'll probably need to change a few things to make his skills good for submission fighting. The first thing I'd teach him is counter-submissions and how to strike.

It's the same with a striker. The big thing is teaching him counter-wrestling—how to counter submissions so he's not going out there, throwing a couple of punches, getting taken down and getting squashed. That happens a lot with good strikers because they're not comfortable on the ground. They get so afraid to throw punches that their timing is off—they don't land their punches.

Another big thing is seeing what kind of shape he's in. Once we get a guy to the point where he's technically good enough with submission, wrestling and striking skills, I'll put him in a straight kickboxing smoker.

BB: Can you define a "smoker"?

Liddell: Basically, it's slang for glorified sparring. It's like a real competition with shin pads, headgear, sparring gloves. ...

BB: But it's not an official fight.

Liddell: It's not official, but it's against another gym. They do the walk-in, and there's usually a small crowd. It simulates the atmosphere of a fight. A lot of guys find out whether or not they want to be out there. Even though it's three two-minute rounds, I guarantee you every guy who goes out there for the first time is going to be pretty damn tired.

BB: Does that help prepare him for five-minute rounds?

Liddell: Yes, especially when you take a wrestler out of his element. Wrestlers are not very comfortable when they can't take a guy down. It

Being kicked and punched is a relatively new experience for wrestlers, says Liddell, so you should accustom yourself to the sensation as quickly as possible.

Photo by Rick Hustead

By themselves, grappling skills are no longer enough to win mixed-martial arts matches, Chuck Liddell (right) says. Everyone also needs to be able to strike.

Photo by Rick Hustead

forces them to strike. But it's no big deal because a loss doesn't count against their record.

BB: How would you improve his conditioning?

Liddell: I'd do a lot of sport-specific stuff and circuit training, hit the weights and hit the bags with running in between. I'd do plyometrics—explosive training with a lot of jumping drills. I'd do sprints and interval work. I don't believe in long-distance running, what old boxers used to do. This isn't a marathon. I'm trying to get explosive power over a period of 15 to 25 minutes. I'm trying to develop his ability to have that explosive power for five minutes, [then] have it again after a one-minute break. I'm not trying to build a powerlifter, a guy who can push a bunch of weight one time. I want him to push a decent amount of weight over a long period of time. So I'd do a lot of explosive stuff with the legs, core-body exercises, jump squats, walking lunges and pilates-type stuff.

BB: Do you have a way of rooting out bad habits in the people you train?

Liddell: It's easier to start with a guy who's never struck before than it is with someone who's been fighting a lot. What happens is you get him all cleaned up in the gym and as soon as the fight starts, it's back to what he

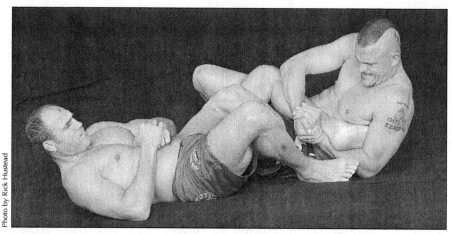

If a fighter is already skilled in grappling, Liddell says he would minimize the training time he devotes to those skills.

Photo by Rick Hustead

knew because the adrenaline's going. A lot of that comes down to keeping an eye on him when he's training. You try to change things over a period of time.

BB: Do you find that fighters learn from their mistakes better when they experience a loss?

Liddell: That's the worst way, but they should learn from every fight they're in. The best ones are the close wins, where they know they didn't fight that well and they made a lot of mistakes, but they got out of it with a win. They do learn a lot from losses because that's when they have to look back and say, What did I do wrong? Usually, I wait a week or so after a fight to talk to my guys about it. I give them a little time—if they won to celebrate, and if they lost to get over it a little bit—before we watch the tape.

BB: What methods do you use to get a fighter to stay on track when he's facing an aggressive opponent?

Liddell: We do a lot of situational stuff, but basically good sparring is where he'll get that. That's why I [mentioned] the smokers—getting a guy who is a wrestler to learn how to strike. If he's doing just mixed-martial arts stuff, a lot of times, as soon as [his opponent] comes in, he's going to take him down, and he'll never learn to strike like that.

BB: How do you prepare a striker to function on the ground?

Liddell: Sometimes it's tougher to teach them the ground stuff, but a lot of guys from boxing have good athletic ability, and it doesn't take long to teach them counter-submissions. They have to be willing to put the time in. They're not going to like it at first because really good boxers are used to winning. They get to [an MMA] gym and there are guys they probably won't be able to beat for two or three months. It's frustrating, but they have to do it.

BB: How do you prepare wrestlers for getting hit?

Liddell: That's one of the hardest things. A lot of wrestlers are gun-shy. Nobody likes getting hit, but it affects wrestlers in a negative way when they're not taking shots well. The only real solution for that is sparring—getting them in there enough so they feel comfortable moving around. There are other things we do: We have a glove on the end of a stick that we use to get them used to being hit and moving out of the way. Sometimes I hit them hard with that glove.

BB: In the education of a fighter, how important is the ability to live with pain?

Liddell: Guys that make it to the top of the sport have gone through a lot of injuries and have been able to push themselves through being hurt in practice. This is one of the hardest sports in the world to train for and not get hurt. I don't think I've gone into a fight at 100 percent in a long, long time. I tell people there are no magic moves that will make them better at this sport. They need to be born with some athletic ability and be able to take a punch. It's hard work.

BB: What importance do you place on image as a factor in a fighter's success?

Liddell: Image plays a bigger role than I would like it to, but promoters want to sell tickets. People have to want to watch the fight. Whether they want to see you lose or win, as long as they want to see you, promoters don't care. It brings in more money.

Don't get me wrong: In this sport, if you're the best in the world, you can still make it as long as you're not losing. But you need to be exciting in the ring and somewhat exciting outside the ring.

BB: What general advice would you give an up-and-coming fighter?

Liddell: Try to finish your fights. When it comes down to it, fans and promoters want guys who try to finish their fights. Even if you win every fight you ever have by decision, as long as you're trying to finish the fight, no one will have a problem with that.

BB: Does finishing a fight include fighting hard even though you're losing?

Liddell: Right. Don't give up in any way and always be trying to win. In some fights, a guy gets a lead and just sits there and holds his opponent. Or in boxing, a guy gets a lead and just dances around for the last two rounds without trying to finish. People don't want to see that.

BB: What can you do to keep a fighter from freezing or losing focus when the lights are bright and the crowd is noisy?

Liddell: The biggest thing is experience. What I try to do the first time they're in a bigger show is get someone they should be able to beat pretty easily. That way, if they do freeze up a little bit, it's not going to cost them the fight. Even guys who freeze up usually settle down after a round. If they lose one round, they have two more to win, so there's time. But if they go out there against an equal and freeze, most likely they're not going to

Photo by Rick Hustead

The only way to learn how to handle the stress of fighting, says Liddell, is to gain experience competing in front of a crowd.

make it out of that first round.

BB: In a fighter's training, how important is sleep?

Liddell: When he's training hard, he needs his sleep because his body needs to recover. I don't worry about sleep when I'm not training, but when I have a fight coming up, I need my sleep.

BB: How does a person's diet change when he's in and out of training?

Liddell: After a fight when I have a little break, I don't worry about what I eat. When I start training again, I start a diet with broader guidelines, but it's a lot cleaner than what I was eating. When I get down to the last eight to 10 weeks and I have to cut my weight, what I eat is very specific.

BB: It's tough enough to monitor yourself, but how do you control the diet of your fighters?

Liddell: It's not easy to eat right. I try to tell them what they should do and try to get them to do it. A lot of them make a good effort, and that's all you need. A few slips here and there aren't going to make a big difference.

BB: Do you have any final advice for aspiring fighters?

Liddell: Find a place that lets you train in everything. Some [coaches] don't want you training with other people and don't want you learning other things. I think you should get with somebody who's not afraid to have you learn from everyone.

Photo by Rick Hustead

Dana White says *The Ultimate Fighter* will hearken back to ancient times when teachers were measured by the ability of their students.

175

MEET THE ULTIMATE FIGHTER!
Diego Sanchez, Poster Boy of the Mixed Martial Arts
by Robert W. Young and Jon Thibault • Photos by Rick Hustead • August 2005

You've got to like a guy who's just proved he's one of the most skilled mixed martial artists in the world, then shyly admits to having Bruce Lee—"He was 50 years ahead of his time"—and Rickson Gracie—"My dream is to roll with him one day if he'll give me the opportunity"—as his role models.

Meet Diego Sanchez, the 23-year-old native of Albuquerque, New Mexico, who commanded four of the most decisive wins seen on Spike TV's *The Ultimate Fighter* reality series. Having been awarded a much-hyped "six-figure contract" with the Ultimate Fighting Championship for his efforts, he's sure to become a familiar face to MMA fans around the world.

Kenpo and Wrestling Roots

Like many *Black Belt* readers, Sanchez got his start in the arts because of the violent environment in which he was raised. "I grew up in a rough neighborhood with a lot of bullies," he says. "It was either fight back against them or get beat up every day."

His parents signed him up for *kenpo* lessons at age 9. He trained for three years and earned his green belt before throwing in the towel. The incident that launched him on the road to MMA stardom was also the straw that broke the camel's back with respect to point karate. "I got screwed at a tournament and cried," he says. "My parents said, 'That's it; we're putting you in wrestling like your cousins.' I was amped to start wrestling because I was very competitive, and I didn't like the point system of karate. When it's in the judges' hands every single time, it's not a real competition."

His enthusiasm would soon hit a snag when the pudgy youth found out he'd be competing against a plethora of conditioned athletes—little though they were. Nevertheless, he managed to win most of the time.

"I kept wrestling and played football in middle school," Sanchez says. "In high school, for the first time in my life, I had to cut weight—which meant I wasn't a chubby kid any more. I went through a tough season getting beat by the varsity guys. There was loss after loss after loss, maybe 15 in a row. It showed me how much I hated to lose, but it set the tone, and I started driving myself to change that. I became a year-round wrestler. I learned how hard I could push my body without breaking. I was getting stronger and faster. I learned how to excel."

In his junior year, Sanchez ruled Albuquerque. He even made it to the semifinals at the New Mexico State Championships. "After doing that, I thought, I can do anything," he says. "The next year, I dominated the competition. I had offers for college scholarships, but I turned them all down because I didn't want to cut weight any more. I was 18 and wanted to grow to my full abilities."

The work ethic he learned and the mind-set he acquired lay the foundation for the success he's enjoying in MMA after such a short time. He now sports an 18-0 record—most of his bouts have been in King of the Cage,

Yoga workouts help Sanchez's strength, flexibility and conditioning. In the future, he hopes to become certified to teach the art.

so the competition has been tough—and he's never been submitted in the ring. "I've done that all in three and a half years," he says. "I view it as a good way to get some experience. I didn't want to jump right in and try to fight the champion. I needed to build myself up. For me, it's all about being well-rounded."

Bigger and Better Things

Sanchez's mission to become well-rounded in MMA took a giant leap forward when he walked into Jackson's Submission Fighting. There, he met Greg Jackson, MMA coach extraordinaire. "I'd been watching the UFC since I was 9—mowing lawns and pulling weeds to get money for the pay-per-view," Sanchez says. "When I walked into Greg's school, I knew about submissions; I just didn't know how to do them. Within two months, I'd won my first tournament."

Sanchez's rapid advances in submission wrestling prompted Jackson to promote him to the intermediate class. "Then I was tapping guys who were advanced, so I went to advanced," he says. "And I kept winning."

In no time, the Sanchez work ethic reared its head again, this time after a couple of serious injuries. He broke his foot while training but opted to continue his workouts whenever possible. "I also had a torn pectoral tendon, but I trained through it," he says. "For three months, I grappled with one arm, and it improved my game tremendously. Some things are blessings in disguise."

In 2003 he went pro. "I was so hungry and driven," he says. "I would do a fight, then do a grappling tournament, then do another fight. For me, as a martial artist, this was my life, my sport and my art."

His quest to continually improve his skills has led him to sample every facet of fighting, then pick his favorites to focus on. "For the ground, I love submission wrestling," he says. "I love ground-and-pound. It's an art."

Early on, Sanchez learned the value of the *muay Thai* offense—the hard way. "I walked into my first professional fight, and the guy, a kickboxer, busted me right in the face," he says. "He hit me so hard, I saw stars. I got cut. Then I went to my corner and thought, Is this really what I want to do for a living? But I had too much pride to let him beat me, so I went back in and choked him out. Then I went home and looked in the mirror and thought, I'm going to have to learn some kickboxing."

Now, he's partial to the knee thrust. "My Thai-boxing instructor, Mike Winklejohn—he's a three-time world champion—and I were doing warm-ups on knees. He said, 'Because of your body style, you have a very powerful

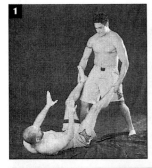
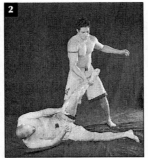

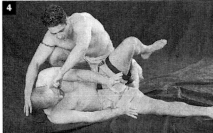

Sanchez controls his opponent's legs (1). He throws them aside (2) before diving in (3) and landing a punch (4). Sanchez then inserts his left arm under the man's arm and around his neck (5). He effects the choke by locking his limbs and squeezing (6).

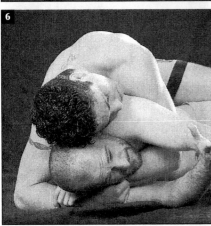

knee.' I learned the technique two days before a fight with a good wrestler. I thought I would try it, and 15 knees later, he was hurting real bad. It worked, and if it works, keep doing it. Being able to grab someone's head and pull his face or ribs into my knee—it's just so effective."

The rest of muay Thai didn't do as much for Sanchez. Its elbow strikes seemed OK, he says, but he preferred plain old punching. He admits to having taken a liking to leg kicks, but pouring any amount of serious time into kick training all too often resulted in his getting sidelined with an injury.

With a taste of Thai-style hand work under his belt, Sanchez did what any self-respecting experimentalist would do: He scheduled himself for a professional boxing match without ever having fought an amateur bout. "I did it because I wanted to have to concentrate on nothing but boxing," he says. "It was fun. It was a good change. I scored a second-round knockout."

In addition to being fun, the bout of pure pugilism taught the budding MMA fighter a valuable lesson: "I found that there's a big difference between boxing and kickboxing. It's in the setups and the footwork. When kicks and knees aren't allowed, it changes everything."

Strategic and Philosophical Principles

Obviously, versatility is required for success in the MMA ring, Sanchez says. But it's not nearly enough. "Nowadays in the UFC, the guys are all

Sanchez sports a body built for the knee thrust, his kickboxing trainer told him.

so well-rounded in grappling, striking and kicking that it comes down to conditioning and heart and who wants it more," he says. "It's also about having your mind, body and spirit in line. And you need a good coach, a good manager and training partners. Even then, it doesn't always go your way. Life is what God gives you."

As soon as he sets foot in the octagon, Sanchez's strategy is simple: Be aggressive. "I believe in animal instinct," he says. "I believe I'm an animal when I get in the ring, and I see my opponent as prey. You may be my friend before a fight, but when the door closes and I'm looking you dead in the eyes, I'm going for the kill. I've said it over and over: I'm a pit bull, and I'll take out the neck—just like an animal in the wild."

Because the specifics of his strategy vary according to the strong points of his opponent's game, it seems only natural that the most challenging matches arise when he's facing someone he has no knowledge of. "It makes you cautious," he says. "You have to respect him because you don't know how good he is. Sometimes you win, and sometimes it's a lesson. You might try to take him down and get kneed in the face. So you try something else."

One thing he advises all would-be champs to get to know up close and personal is what it feels like to get hit in the head. "Like in anything, you have to work your way up," he says. "Buy a pair of 16-ounce gloves and some headgear. Find an opponent who's at your level or maybe a little below it—you're not going in there to knock his head off. You'll find that getting hit in the head is the same whether your eyes are open or closed. So keep your eyes open and see that punch coming. Feel it. The next time, it won't be so bad. Then work your way up with someone who's a little tougher and hits a little harder."

Once you've become intimate with pain, it's time to work on your mental attributes, Sanchez says. "Because it's a game of chess in the ring, I'm big on meditation. I visualize my hand getting raised in victory. I visualize the fans. I visualize hugging my mom afterward. I visualize every part of the fight, every technique. It makes your mind that much faster because you've already gone through it. It's like doing your homework in college and then getting a job. You're better prepared than the competition."

Strength and Conditioning Secrets

When it comes to training, Sanchez says he'll try any kind of workout. "And I'll have fun doing it. A while ago, I took up break dancing as a hobby—and for strength conditioning, flexibility and agility. It's fun, and

Sanchez holds his opponent in his guard (1). Sanchez shifts his opponent's right arm to the side (2) and begins maneuvering out from under him (3). Once he gets to the man's back (4), Sanchez wraps his right arm around his neck (5) and sinks in the rear-naked choke (6).

it teaches you how to move and generate power from any position. Dancing is about rhythm, and fighting has a lot to do with rhythm. If you can incorporate that into your mind, you can fight better."

Until a recent injury, he honed his cardio by running hills and mountains near his hometown in the Southwest. Now he relies on other methods—including dancing and yoga, which bolsters conditioning, strength and flexibility. To build his muscles and joints, he concentrates on free-weight exercises. "The joints are the weakest part of the body, and you're only as strong as your weakest part," he says. "To strengthen them, I do rehabilitation-therapy exercises, like the ones you do when you're hurt. Then I just increase the weight and reps when I need to."

But when he's ready to get down to business, Sanchez is a firm believer in specificity of training. "To condition myself for a fight, I do grappling and fighting," he says. "I go round after round—what we call the Circle of Death. There are 12 guys, and after every five minutes, you get a fresh guy. You only get a one-minute break."

To survive pseudo death matches like that, a fighter needs to be able to see an opportunity and seize it, he says. To do that, he has to be fluent in the techniques and have established the muscle memory that comes from having done them thousands of times. "The opening lasts only a fraction of a second, then it's gone," he says. "You have to go for it."

Go for it is exactly what Sanchez did in every bout he competed in on *The Ultimate Fighter* and in King of the Cage before that. Despite the massacres he inflicted on his opponents, success hasn't swelled his head. "I'm still a student," he says. "I know what I know, but I'm still learning. I don't believe in reaching a peak. I think you can always get better. My goal is to be the most well-rounded fighter in the world. I have the assets. I'm open-minded, and with that mentality, I'm going all the way to the top."

And after that? "When I retire, I want to run a school and teach," he says. "I want to get certified in yoga and teach that, also. But before then—probably within the next year or two—you'll see me in some fight scenes in movies. But I'm not trying to become some big actor; I'm concentrating on fighting because that's what I'm best at."

Welcome to My Nightmare

Black Belt: In *The Ultimate Fighter,* did you change your game plan depending on whether you faced a wrestler like Josh Koscheck or a *jujutsu* stylist like Kenny Florian?

Diego Sanchez: Every fight has a different game plan. With Koscheck, it was a lot different. I'd gone day in and day out for 60 days, teaching him everything I knew to help his game. We would train hard against each other and make each other better. It was awkward. We were best friends and training partners, but then it was like: "OK, it's business. I know I want it more than you do."

BB: It must have been difficult because you'd taught him defenses to many of your moves.

Sanchez: Exactly. In the last couple of weeks of training, I realized he was really susceptible to the guillotine, and I hadn't been using it on him. I got him once or twice in practice with it. Then I got him in a guillotine at the very end of the first round [of our fight], and it would have been another five grand for me if I'd had just two more seconds.

BB: Prior to fighting Kenny Florian in the season finale, you thought he would be one of your toughest opponents. During the match, however, he didn't seem to pose much of a challenge. What do you think he did wrong?

183

Sanchez: I don't think it's necessarily what he did wrong; I think it's what I did right. Kenny's an awesome fighter, and a lot of guys on the show even thought that he was going to out-strike me. He prepared for me by working his *muay Thai* and boxing a lot, but he didn't train with a 230-pound guy on top of him the way I did. I have a great team, and I have excellent teammates. I knew he didn't have anybody to really put it to him the way I did.

When I was going into the finals, I knew we were both very good grapplers, but there was a difference: I could take him down, and he couldn't take me down. I knew I was going to be on top, throwing the leather. And that's exactly what happened. I didn't expect it to go so good.

BB: Was it strange to fight in front of so many people?

Sanchez: I had fought in front of 8,000 people before, and the [finale of *The Ultimate Fighter*] was in front of about 3,000. The crowds help me—

In MMA competition, Sanchez draws mostly from submission wrestling, boxing and muay Thai.

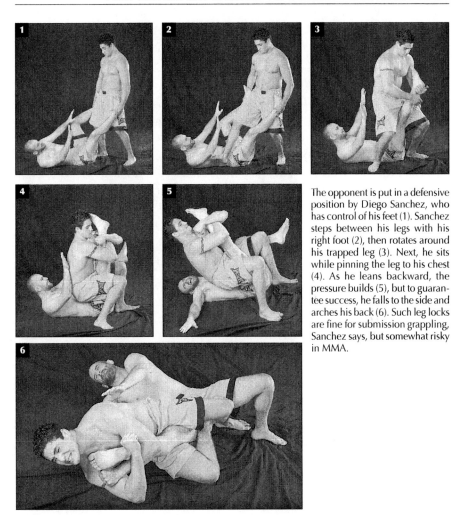

The opponent is put in a defensive position by Diego Sanchez, who has control of his feet (1). Sanchez steps between his legs with his right foot (2), then rotates around his trapped leg (3). Next, he sits while pinning the leg to his chest (4). As he leans backward, the pressure builds (5), but to guarantee success, he falls to the side and arches his back (6). Such leg locks are fine for submission grappling, Sanchez says, but somewhat risky in MMA.

hearing my fans and my family screaming for me, giving me their energy. Before I got out there, when I was in the warm-up room, my muscles were tired and I felt like crap. As soon as I walked out and heard those mariachis and the crowd going crazy for me, I felt like I was a lightning bolt.

BB: You seem to favor the rear-naked choke. Is that something you consciously go for?

Sanchez: I'm very good at getting to [my opponent's] back, and I've evolved the choke a little bit. The way I get there has evolved, the way I put it on has evolved and the way I finish it has evolved. I looked at the counters, and I rethought the move. I took a little from the top Brazilian-jujutsu guys and submission wrestlers.

BB: On the show, you were really into pre-fight meditation—absorbing energy from the storm clouds and so forth. Was it tough to get your game on with all the cameras and people around?

Sanchez: That stuff doesn't bother me. I zone it all out, and it's like being alone. It's a meditative state. My career is my life, and my family and all of this is at stake. So every fight I go into, I have that ultimate fear of losing. I use the nickname "Nightmare" because before every fight, I get these horrible nightmares about losing, and it gives me a taste of what it would feel like. And it's so real—I'll be sleeping and wake up, and I'll go back to sleep to try to finish the fight. I had this dream one time where I lost a fight to Dan Severn, and it was the worst feeling ever. It was so real.

BB: What weight will you fight at in the UFC?

Sanchez: I plan on fighting my first three or four fights at 170 pounds— as long as it takes to get to Matt Hughes if he's still the champ. I'm going to be ready for whoever they put in front of me.

BB: After that, do you plan on going back up to 185 pounds and winning that weight class?

Sanchez: Yeah. I'm 23 years old. I won't stop filling in until I'm 28. I want to fight the bigger men. I'm good enough to fight them.

The show and the fights I've had up until now are just a prelude, just a little intro to what's to come in the future. Mark my words: I'm going to be the UFC champ at 170 and at 185. My goal was to win the show, come into the UFC, be the most marketable person the UFC has ever seen, and cater to the Hispanic and Latino fans of boxing who haven't come over to mixed martial arts yet. There are millions of them, and they haven't crossed over yet. My goal is to bring those people to MMA, grow our sport and dominate in the UFC.

THE TWISTER
Eddie Bravo Speaks Out on His Signature Technique, Grappling With and Without a Gi, and His Victory Over Royler Gracie

Interview by Jon Thibault • Photos by Rick Hustead • November 2005

"According to an ancient Sumerian text, the oldest version of the Bible, there is a 10th planet in our solar system called Nibiru where a highly advanced humanlike civilization lives. Their jujutsu must be off the hook."

—*Eddie Bravo*

Black Belt: When people refer to the "Eddie Bravo style of jujutsu," what do they mean?

Eddie Bravo: Right now, it's an unorthodox style, but I think it's unorthodox only because it's new. I've concentrated on setting up submissions from overhooks and underhooks, and I've been doing that for so long that it's become my style—not just using tie-ups for defense, but working offense off them, too.

I've taken Machado jujutsu and geared it toward no-*gi* grappling. That's the problem with [Brazilian] jujutsu: Guys spend all their time training in a gi, and they get used to holding the sleeve and the collar to set everything up. But if you take the gi off, you take away their fighting stance and all the setups.

I saw early in the Ultimate Fighting Championship that the jujutsu guys would have dudes in their guard, but they'd never sweep them or go for finishes. I thought, What's going on? Why aren't they doing armbars and triangles? Why aren't they sweeping?

They were just defending in the guard. The reason became clear after thinking about it for a while—it was the gi. You can't just switch [to no-gi techniques] overnight. You have to master those overhooks and underhooks, and that takes a long time.

BB: So that's when you decided to specialize in no-gi grappling?

Bravo: It was more important for my jujutsu to be effective without the gi because I knew there was a chance that I would do some mixed martial arts. I wanted to start with jujutsu that was as MMA-ready as possible, and that meant not using the collar or sleeves to set everything up. I started training like that with a gi around 1996. I purposely wouldn't grab the collar or sleeve. I would use head control or overhooks. I knew that, one day, no-gi would become popular. It was obvious that no-gi was the future—it's just a lot more fun. Gi tournaments are just a bore-fest tug of war [with] people barely moving. People are starting to realize that it's about grappling, not about this Japanese superhero outfit.

BB: Where does your nickname, "The Twister," come from?

Bravo: I made the wrestler's guillotine—which is now called the twister—work in jujutsu. A lot of jujutsu guys think I made up that move, but wrestlers knew what it was. It's a very dramatic hold, probably the craziest-looking submission out there. Most of the time when I competed,

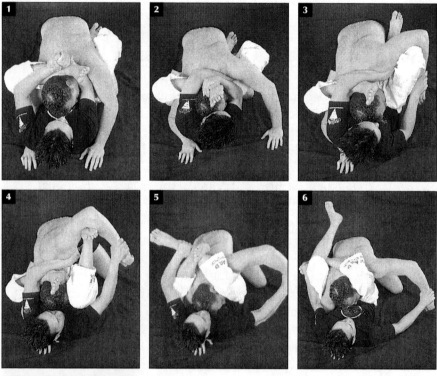

The meat hook: Eddie Bravo (bottom) controls his opponent by placing his right foot on his left hip and wrapping his left leg and arms around his neck (1). He then uses his right hand to hold his own foot so he can slide his left hand into the opponent's left armpit (2). Next, Bravo secures the man's left arm by holding the wrist with his right hand, which allows him to reposition his right leg (3) until his foot can be used to momentarily push against the opponent's left biceps (4). Bravo's right leg moves across the opponent's back until he can grab it with his left hand (5). To finish, he locks his right foot behind his left knee (6) and completes the triangle choke (7).

THE ULTIMATE GUIDE TO MIXED MARTIAL ARTS

I made sure I did the twister instead of just going for armbars and triangles like everyone else. I wanted to capture a lot of twisters on video to flip people out.

BB: A lot of people assume their submission vocabulary increases with a gi. Is that correct?

Bravo: Technically, there might be more moves you can do with a gi, but a lot of submissions are easier without a gi—any kind of choke, the arm triangle and the inverted arm triangle, for example. All of those slip in tighter with sweat and grease.

The Brazilians say, "In order to be good without a gi, you have to train with a gi." Everyone believes that. It's the craziest thing. It's like this blind allegiance to this cloth that [the Brazilians] made sacred. That's like saying, "In order to get good at Greco-Roman wrestling, you have to train in judo first," and that's not true.

If you want to be a great baseball player, you have to start playing in Little League. If you want to be a pro boxer, you have to start boxing when you're 12 or 13. It's just like no-gi grappling. It's so new right now that people don't know whether to use a gi. But eventually no-gi jujutsu, submission wrestling, or whatever you want to call it will end up just like all other sports: If you want to be a champion, you'd better start when you're eight, and you'd better not use a gi.

BB: Do you think no-gi jujutsu should be classified as its own sport?

Bravo: Give it 25 or 30 years, and it'll become really clear. If you want to be a champion at this sport, you're going to not bother with a gi. But right now, nobody sees that. When kickboxing blew up in the late '60s and early '70s, most of the kickboxers had a karate background. But we know now that if you want to be a K-1 champion, a karate background isn't necessary. The best thing to do is take a 12-year-old kid and start him right away with *muay Thai* techniques. It's the same with no-gi jujutsu.

BB: At your school, 10th Planet Jiu Jitsu, do you train only without a gi?

Bravo: Yes. If you want to be a gi champion, train in a gi. But for me, it's more important if my students are not those guys who have been training in jujutsu for 10-plus years, then take off their gi and don't have much offense. That would be embarrassing to me. I want my students to be really good at submitting people with no gi.

If they were to put on a gi for some crazy reason and get tapped out a million times, that wouldn't bother me. What means more is a guy who can pull it off in MMA. It means you're better at jujutsu.

BB: Could you run our readers through your match with Royler Gracie at the 2003 ADCC Submission Wrestling World Championship?

Bravo: I was pretty confident going into that fight because I'd just beaten a Brazilian world champion in the match before. I felt like I could beat [Royler]. Once the match started, he was a lot better than I thought. I thought I'd go through him quickly, but his technique was good, and it took a while for me to pull anything off. He was controlling me pretty well. He didn't ever have me in any offensive danger, but he was very hard to control and maneuver, and it was hard for me to put him into full-guard. Once I finally got him into full-guard, that's when I went to work. He wasn't used to my guard techniques. He'd never seen that before, and he was kind of confused, kind of frustrated.

BB: In that match, you used the "rubber guard." Please explain what that is.

Bravo: It's just playing high-guard without a gi. With a gi, when you're playing high-guard, you're in an offensive position. You're trying to get an armbar or triangle. It's easy to play high-guard with a gi because your legs stick up there. It's not slippery. But without a gi, it's hard to play high-guard, so it's hard to be offensive.

So what I do is hold up my legs with my wrists and arms. I hook my own ankles to keep my legs up there. If I let my ankles go, my legs slip down because of all the sweat. I developed a way of playing high-guard while holding up my legs with one of my arms and then setting up a submission with my other arm. That's the basis of my guard.

So I was setting up Royler with the rubber guard. He was confused. He knew I wanted an *oma plata* on his right side, so he kind of over-defended on that side. He broke through the rubber guard, passed it for an instant, then I put him back in the guard using this move I call "the jailbreak." He wasn't used to people recovering like I did. He passed my guard maybe three times for a second, and I recovered quickly using my flexibility. I knew he'd never seen that before because he wasn't even trying to stop it.

I had an overhook on his right side, and I faked a sweep, put him right into the butterfly guard and then—bam!—grabbed his wrist, threw my right leg over and finished in a triangle. I kept thinking, Wow, I've got this guy! When someone's caught in my triangle, he's done. I freaked out a little bit because I was running out of time, so I squeezed as hard as I could. I finally pulled down on his head, and he tapped.

BB: How did you start in jujutsu?

Bravo: I'm actually a musician. I've been in bands all my life. I play drums and the guitar. I moved to Hollywood to seek out my rock-star dreams. I knew I had to be in shape, so I joined a gym—and I hated it. I'd always been a Bruce Lee fanatic, and I always wanted to do the martial arts as a kid, but I could never afford it. I joined a karate school when I was 22. After a year of karate, I saw the Ultimate Fighting Championship and was blown away by what Royce Gracie was doing. I was like, "I've got to do jujutsu."

I'd wrestled for two years in high school, and I thought, Jujutsu is kind

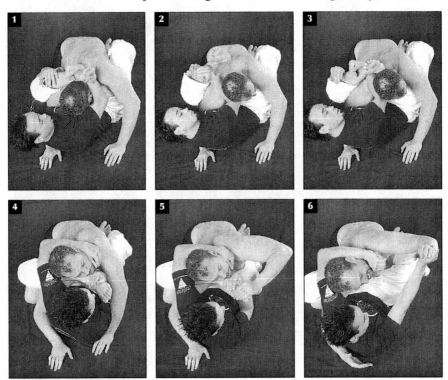

The loco plata: Bravo holds Laurence Zwirn in the New York position, trapping his right hand on the mat (1). He clears the opponent's neck with his right arm (2), then underhooks his own left ankle and hugs his knee with his left arm (3). Next, Bravo pulls his left foot in front of the opponent's face and squeezes his head with his left arm (4). The opponent attempts to counter by pushing Bravo's foot away from his face (5), but Bravo counters the counter by grabbing the man's left wrist (6). To execute the finishing move, Bravo uses his left hand to push his left foot up, then boosts the pressure on the opponent's neck by using his right foot to push against his left heel (7).

191

of like wrestling. I'd never thought of wrestling as a martial art; I thought that you were supposed to stay on your feet in a real fight and that going to the ground was cheating. In high school, whenever anybody got in my face, I would just take him down, get side control and punch him in the stomach. I was the original ground-and-pounder! How ironic is that?

When I saw what Royce was doing, I quit karate. I wanted to start jujutsu

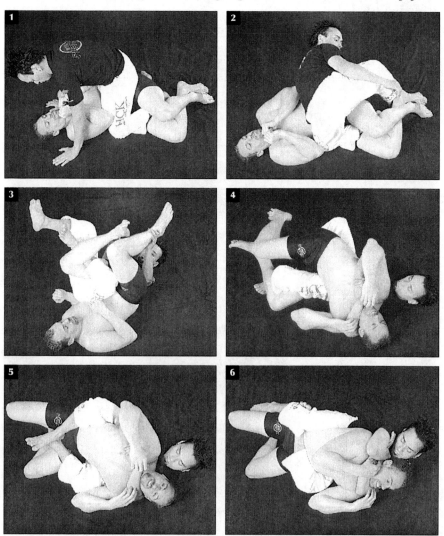

The samurai: Bravo begins in his opponent's quarter-guard with his left foot trapped (1). He starts to spin clockwise (2), then rolls on his left shoulder toward the man's back (3). Bravo maneuvers his left arm over the opponent's left shoulder and his right arm under the opponent's right arm before clasping his hands (4). Next, he places his right leg hook around the man's torso (5) and fastens the anaconda body triangle as he completes the rear-naked choke (6).

right away but couldn't afford it, so I joined a Dan Inosanto protégé academy called the Magda Institute—a little *jeet kune do,* a little muay Thai, a little *kali.* So for about six months, I did that system, then I started making more money and joined Jean-Jacques Machado's jujutsu club. I decided to do both: jujutsu once a week and two days of striking at the Magda Institute. I bumped it up from once a week to twice a week and got addicted. I couldn't wait to get to jujutsu. I would run red lights. I would be in a frantic rage to get to class. I eventually dedicated all my time to jujutsu.

BB: Where do you see jujutsu going in the next decade? Do think there will be a complete separation between gi and no-gi practice?

Bravo: I think so. I think the no-gi part of grappling is definitely going to take over once people realize they don't have to wear this crazy Japanese outfit. At my school, you can wear whatever you want. It's about respecting one another, listening to the instructor and having fun. It's about the grappling, not about what outfit you wear.

BB: Do you have any closing comments?

Bravo: My book is coming out soon. It's the first jujutsu book to come out on a major label. It's from McGraw-Hill. It'll be in bookstores across the country.

BB: Will the twister be in there?

Bravo: Everything will be in there.

ARMLESS ARM LOCKS
On the Mat With Gokor Chivichyan
by S.D. Seong • Photos by Rick Hustead • January 2006

Gokor Chivichyan is a martial artist who needs no introduction—but he'll get one anyway. Inducted into the *Black Belt* Hall of Fame in 1997 as Judo Instructor of the Year, he made a name for himself first in his native Armenia, then in the former Soviet Union and Europe. He moved to the United States in 1981 and immediately started putting his judo and *sambo* knowledge to good use. Shortly thereafter, he hooked up with "Judo" Gene LeBell, and the two have led the submission-grappling world ever since.

Chivichyan has appeared in *Black Belt* numerous times over the years to share the knowledge he's gleaned from decades of training, teaching and competing, but this time it's for something unique. His objective is to pass along six methods for executing an arm lock *without using your*

Gokor Chivichyan (right) faces his opponent (1). The opponent shoots in for a takedown (2), and Chivichyan controls his upper body while dropping his weight onto his back (3). The grappling expert then uses his left leg to extend the man's arm (4) before locking it in place with his legs and applying downward pressure with his pelvis (5).

To escape from the armbar depicted above, the opponent angles his forearm backward (1-2). Gokor Chivichyan unlocks his ankles (3) and traps the man's limb in the crook of his knee (4). The submission is effected when he twists his hips to straighten the arm (5). Note how he uses his right hand to prevent the opponent from moving his body to relieve the pressure.

arms. Now, most grapplers can rattle off a number of arm torques and twists that will tap out their opponent: the armbar, the *kimura*, the top wrist lock and so on. But without exception, they all involve using your hands or arms to apply pressure to your opponent's limb. Not so with the techniques Chivichyan is teaching here.

Browse through the following pages and practice the moves when you have a chance. Try them on the mat until they're second nature. If you're comfortable using them, feel free to spring one on your adversary in competition; he probably won't know what hit him. And even if you don't like them, tuck them away in the back of your mind, because you never know when you might have to use one of them when either your arm or shoulder is injured and giving up is not an option.

The opponent (top) is controlled by Gokor Chivichyan (1). The grappling teacher maneuvers his left leg (2-4) until he can position himself near the opponent's extended left arm (5). Next, he swings his right leg over the trapped arm (6) and sits up (7). A shift of Chivichyan's body causes the man to tap (8).

Gokor Chivichyan holds his opponent in the scarf-hold position (1). He extends his trapped arm (2) and uses his leg to immobilize it (3). Chivichyan completes the submission technique by applying downward pressure with his left leg and upward pressure with his right (4).

SHOOTFIGHTING VS. MIXED MARTIAL ARTS
MMA Fans Should Know the Difference!

by Bart Vale • Photos by Richard Gardner • February 2006

Often when you're watching a televised martial arts event like the Ultimate Fighting Championship or PRIDE, you'll hear an announcer refer to a competitor as a shootfighter. Then, moments later, you might hear the announcer say the same fighter does the mixed martial arts.

Shootfighting ... mixed martial arts ... shootfighting ... mixed martial arts. ...

What most announcers—and even some people who claim to do shootfighting—don't realize is that the two terms aren't the same. Shootfighting is a distinct system that was developed in Japan long before the UFC popular-

Against a wrestler seeking to effect a tackle, shootfighter Bart Vale (left) can employ a knee strike.

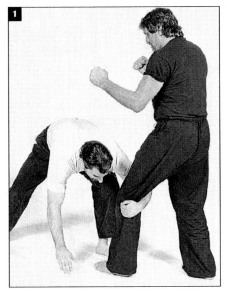

The opponent initiates a single-leg takedown (1). Vale lifts the grabbed leg while pivoting counterclockwise (2). The action catches the man's arm in the crook of Vale's left knee and scissors it against his right thigh. Keeping the arm trapped between his legs, Vale drops his weight to the ground and applies pressure by lifting upward and inward with his left leg (3).

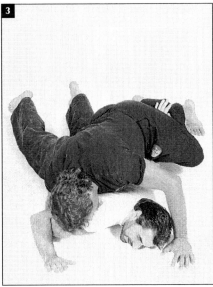

ized the idea of MMA competition. The philosophy behind it was to create a style that merges stand-up techniques with submission wrestling.

In contrast, what you find in many schools that teach MMA is an instructor who shows you striking techniques one night and ground techniques the next. While that's OK and a number of good schools use this method, it can leave a big gap in the student's training—namely, how to transition from the stand-up position to the ground.

Curriculum Problems

At most schools that divide their MMA curriculum into stand-up days and grappling days, lessons in ground work begin with both fighters kneeling or lying down. Although it's often done to promote safety and simplify the teaching process, it's not the most realistic way to practice. It's essential for students to learn how to take their opponent down and how to protect themselves as a fight transitions from stand-up to the ground.

According to a recent news report, a leading ground-fighting expert got into a street fight and tried to perform a leg tackle on his adversary. Unfortunately, they were fighting on concrete, and the ground fighter reportedly broke his own knee while attempting the takedown. The old saying that 90 percent of fights end up on the ground may be true, but it's also true that 100 percent of fights start while standing up.

Knowledge of the proper way to transition from striking to the ground is the component that many MMA practitioners lack. Even schools that include wrestling techniques along with their striking and ground work sometimes fail to teach students how to properly incorporate this important aspect of combat.

Superior Training

In the early days of shootfighting in the United States, many outstanding amateur wrestlers tried to become involved in the sport to make some money in Japan. Although they were skilled at takedowns, more than a few didn't survive the first training session because as they would shoot in for a leg tackle, they would be greeted with a knee to the face. The result: instant knockout.

What the wrestlers—and many of today's MMA practitioners—failed to anticipate was the need to adjust their techniques and strategies for a different set of circumstances. In amateur wrestling, no one is allowed to knee, kick or punch you as you attempt to perform your takedown. Likewise, boxers and kickboxers don't have to worry about someone tackling them when they strike. Even though practicing one aspect of fighting at a time—that is, only striking, only takedowns or only ground work—can make training simpler, it also tends to develop bad habits that leave the fighter vulnerable to unexpected attacks.

Instead of breaking down the curriculum into its striking component, its takedown component and its grappling component, shootfighting instructors prefer to combine the three elements as much as possible. In a shootfighting gym, freestyle grappling usually starts in a stand-up position with some light striking incorporated. That way, students learn the proper way to adjust their takedowns, positioning themselves so they don't have to absorb any unnecessary punishment while they try to maneuver their opponent to the ground. This method also allows for something unique in shootfighting: the ability to defend against a strike by going directly into a submission hold.

As the opponent executes a right-leg roundhouse kick, Vale blocks with his left forearm (1). He then reaches over the extended leg with his right arm (2). As he wraps his right hand over his left wrist, he uses his left hand to grip the man's foot near the toes (3). Next, the shootfighter drops his weight forward, forcing the opponent to the ground where he can be submitted with an ankle lock (4). The key to applying pressure is to push forward with the left hand while rotating the opponent's toes toward his buttocks.

Most ground-fighting arts require that both practitioners be on the mat before a submission technique can be applied. Shootfighting instructors, in contrast, teach numerous holds—including defenses against punches, kicks and takedowns—that begin in the standing position and finish on the ground. Essential to their successful execution is a smooth transition from striking to grappling range.

Mastering that transition requires developing an awareness of what strikers, wrestlers and ground fighters can and can't do. Once you understand that kickboxers tend to overcommit during their roundhouse kicks, putting all their momentum behind them, you can learn how to catch

Vale's adversary attacks with a roundhouse kick to the body, and Vale tucks his hips back to lessen the impact (1). The shootfighter then uses his arms to trap the leg against his midsection (2). Holding the leg tight, Vale begins to arch backward (3), and as he falls, he spins to his left (4). Continuing the turn, Vale rolls the opponent onto his side (5). He finishes with a shin lock, which is effected by keeping his right elbow braced against the inner part of the opponent's lower right leg and pushing down between the shin and calf while lifting the foot (6, reverse view).

the attacking limb and quickly move into a leg lock while your opponent attempts to remain balanced. Once you understand that wrestlers sometimes reach around your leg to execute a grab prior to a takedown, you can use it against them by scissoring the offending arm and trapping it there. By the same token, you'll also learn to not do those things when you attack.

Anything Goes

One type of training shootfighters often use is to put on boxing gloves, shin pads and headgear, then spar full contact with grappling techniques. That enables the fighter with good stand-up skills to make a grappler pay for trying poorly executed techniques. Although wearing gloves makes it more challenging for the grappler to perform takedowns and submissions, he becomes better at avoiding knockouts as he attempts his ground techniques.

No-holds-barred competitions have already shined a spotlight on the importance of being knowledgeable in all areas of fighting. But now, practitioners have to learn how to transcend *mixed* martial arts and become *complete* martial artists. It's one thing to know how to strike, wrestle and do submissions; it's another thing altogether to be able to blend those techniques and strategies in the ring.

NO BARRIERS
Randy Couture's Prescription for Peak Performance for Middle-Aged Martial Artists

by Jatinder Dhoot • Photo by Rick Hustead • March 2006

When Randy Couture enters the octagon to face Chuck Liddell on February 4, 2006, first-time viewers will be shocked to read over the Tale of the Tape graphic and see that Couture is 42. The conditioning that "The Natural" displays in his fights would be admirable for an athlete in his 20s, but it's simply phenomenal for a man in his 40s.

Rising to and staying at that level isn't easy for anyone. Plenty of regimentation with respect to diet, exercise and recovery time is required. Over the years, Couture has discovered through trial and error what kind of training and preparation best prepares his body for the octagon. This interview will shine a spotlight on some of those winning methods.

Black Belt: What essential exercises do you use to improve your cardio for your Ultimate Fighting Championship bouts?

Randy Couture: Outside of sparring, which is a huge factor for cardio ability, I do strength training. And I try to simulate the fight and the duration of the fight as much as possible, so I break my sprint routine down into five five-minute "rounds." I give myself a minute break between rounds just like in a fight.

BB: During a match, do you employ any between-round routines to make sure you have enough fuel to keep going?

Couture: The first thing my corner tries to do when I come back is force me to breathe—take deep breaths and get a good oxygen exchange going. In most cases, I prefer to stand between rounds because when you sit, your heart rate drops much faster, and when you stand back up to engage again, it's a more drastic contrast. Standing, your heart rate settles more naturally and you stay in the position that you want to be in when you step back out to fight. And it's easier to breathe in the standing position than it is in the sitting position.

BB: Do you have to make an effort to think about your breathing during matches?

Couture: I usually don't, but I know people who do have that problem—especially while flurrying their punches, they hold their breath. When you start throwing combinations and end up holding your breath for 20 or 30 seconds, it can really affect you. You have to consciously remember to breathe. One thing that can be done is to make a noise when you breathe and make that conscious. Then, once you've created the rhythm, subconsciously you'll begin to breathe on your own without having to make the noise.

BB: Does running help you improve your cardio?

Couture: That's something that's contrary to what we're led to believe. We're used to boxers who do miles and miles and miles of roadwork. I don't do that because I don't think it's in line with this sport. There's nothing slow and long about fighting. That's why there's sprint training, which my runs consist of. A couple of days a week, I do sprints on the treadmill because that simulates what I encounter: short bursts of 20 seconds to a minute over the period of the fight. Unless you have a weight problem and are trying to burn extra calories and body fat, long runs don't serve any purpose.

BB: You seem to be getting stronger with age. To what do you attribute that?

Couture: I've gotten smarter in designing my training tactics and training techniques, and I've learned to listen to my body more. I've learned to make sure I get more rest and taper properly so I can peak for a fight. All those things play into being in better shape. Some think more is better, but that's not always the case. You can spar too hard and too often without giving your body time to rest and recover.

BB: What advice would you give fighters in their late 30s and early 40s who are looking to improve their conditioning in the ring?

Couture: You need a regular routine to maintain your fitness level. The biggest thing that helps me is that I'm able to be in a gym a lot on a daily basis, and that keeps my fitness level pretty broad and high and allows me to peak. I know that I, as an athlete, can't afford to take a month or two off and not do anything. We don't have that luxury as we get older, so maintaining our fitness routine even when we don't have a fight staring us in the face is very important.

BB: What do you adhere to in terms of diet?

Couture: My normal eating habits don't change when I'm peaking, but I do get a little bit stricter. Several months before a fight, I'm still eating a lot of greens, still trying to stay away from sugars, processed foods and dairy products. During the stage of training when I'm just learning new skills and developing new techniques and tactics and maintaining my fitness level, a cookie now and then isn't going to kill me, and having a beer with dinner isn't going to kill me. But that's something I wouldn't do in that 10-week period before a fight. I live by the 80-20 rule: 80 percent of the time I'm on track and doing exactly what I want to do, and 20 percent of the time I live a little and enjoy all the things that I get exposed to. But I'm still heading in the right direction.

BB: As you moved down to the light-heavyweight class, did your cardio improve?

Couture: I don't know if my cardio improved, but I definitely felt more agile and mobile.

BB: Have you ever run out of gas in a bout?

Couture: The only time I really felt that way was against Pedro Rizzo in our first fight [in the UFC 31]. I gave everything I had in that first round to finish it. I was sure John [McCarthy] was going to stop the bout. With about 20 seconds left in the round, I realized he wasn't going to stop it and I had basically punched myself out. I had to get up and try to recover in a minute, then come back out and find a way to finish the fight—and I was pretty damn tired.

In my last fight with Mike Van Arsdale [in the UFC 54], I felt a lot more fatigued than I'm used to. Part of that was due to the infection I had and the high-powered antibiotics I took the week before. I felt I was struggling against myself in that fight. When I watched it on tape, it didn't really show, but I certainly felt a difference.

BB: Are wrestling scrambles like the ones you got into with Van Arsdale very tiring?

Couture: Yes. You're both expending a lot of energy, and there's constant action and motion. It's tit for tat, move for move, trying to catch the other guy out of position so you can gain an advantage. Psychologically and physically, it can be very tiring. I also think that throwing a big flurry of punches to hurt somebody or finish a fight can be tiring. You have to make sure your shots are counting and you're not blowing your energy because you still might have to finish the fight.

BB: When you fought Tito Ortiz in the UFC 44, you had him in some bad positions but John McCarthy didn't stop the bout. Did you have to make a conscious effort not to punch yourself out?

Couture: Absolutely. I had Tito mounted in the fourth round, I think, and I was landing some shots on him. But he was defending himself and managed to recover well. I could have easily taken that next step and spent some energy to try to finish the fight, but I had to consciously decide if I was being effective. Was I landing shots to finish the fight? And I had to hold back.

BB: Do you believe fighters with a strong wrestling background are the best-conditioned athletes in the mixed martial arts?

Couture: I don't know if in general they're the best conditioned, but most wrestlers come from a very professional training environment, so they're exposed to coaches who put them through specific training to get them in shape and ready for peak performance. They understand hard training and how to get the most out of themselves. It's very important in a fight to take that knowledge and [use it to] prepare. A lot of other athletes who fight don't have any idea about that. They're not sure how to put all the pieces of the puzzle together to ensure peak performance.

BB: How can a fighter who's beginning to run out of gas conserve energy and continue the match?

Couture: You've got to find ways to change the position so you can rest and recover and recuperate. Afterward, you need to go back and evaluate your training, learn what put you in that position. Sometimes it's just as much mental as it is physical. Guys often mentally expend a lot of energy before the fight. They get caught up in the hype and all the things that go along with fighting, and then they have less of a tank when it comes time to actually compete. So some guys get nerves or whatever you want to call it. Maybe it's because they're doing the wrong kind of training, or maybe they're overtraining. But you definitely have to find out because your conditioning and approach are two of the few things in a fight that you have control over.

THE PRIDE OF PRIDE
The Techniques, Tactics and Training of
Welterweight Champion Dan Henderson
Interview by Lito Angeles • Photos by Rick Hustead • August 2006

*D*an Henderson is an oddity in the world of the mixed martial arts. He's *rather average-looking compared to the pumped-up specimens that populate his world, and he confesses that he's not flexible enough to touch his own toes. Yet for the past few years, he's been a force to be reckoned with in the PRIDE ring, earning himself an overall record of 20-4. A former Olympic wrestler, the 35-year-old Oregonian has cross-trained himself onto the welterweight throne of Japan's biggest mixed-martial arts promotion. More than anything else, Henderson brings his fists to his fights, but as you'll see, there's much more to this elite combat athlete than meets the eye.*

—Editor

Black Belt: In the mixed martial arts, cardio is obviously important. Are your workouts more focused on long-distance training or sprint training?

Dan Henderson: I mix it up. I probably need to do a little more cross-training to up my cardio. I don't run [a lot] because of my back. I do sprints, go mountain biking and stuff like that. I also do box-hops [plyometrics].

BB: Do you follow a set regimen for the plyometrics?

Henderson: It varies. I usually go for a minute on and 30 seconds off. I do one exercise about eight to 10 times, then another exercise eight to 10 times. Then I do some sprints, sometimes with a bungee, for whatever length the mat is—usually 75 feet.

BB: Do you also use focus pads in your cardio training?

Henderson: Yes. When I do those workouts, I do at least three-minute rounds, sometimes five-minute rounds.

BB: Do you have a set routine, or do you do whatever you decide on that particular day?

Henderson: It's whatever I want to work on on that day. If I want to work on combinations or something, I do them a little more. Then I might hit the bag for a couple of rounds, the focus mitts for three or four rounds, and the bag for three or four rounds.

BB: Are your workouts more power- or speed-oriented? When you hit the bag, are you just trying to blast through it, or do you do rapid-fire punches?

Henderson: I try to speed my punches up as much as I can, but most of the time I try to go hard, as well. The difficult thing is to throw really hard and not telegraph the punch.

BB: With strength and weight training, are you a believer in low repetitions with high weight or a lot of reps with moderate weight?

Henderson: High reps with low weight. In some workouts, I do 20 to 30 reps in my low-rep workout. Right now, I'm doing one set of 100 reps for 13 to 14 exercises. I go through it as fast as I can.

BB: Is it a circuit?

Henderson: It's a circuit with machine weights. I get the weight to where I can do 60 to 70 reps nonstop. Then if I have to stop, I stop for 10 seconds and finish it. It helps with muscle endurance, and it makes me stronger. I

don't think it would do me a lot of good to max out after three to five reps. I want to make sure my muscles are still there after 19 minutes [of fighting].

BB: Do other mixed martial artists train like that?

Henderson: I don't know how other fighters train, but I'm sure that some of them do. I'm not saying my way is right or wrong; it works for me.

BB: What about flexibility? Do you spend a lot of time stretching?

Henderson: I haven't really done much stretching in the past 15 years. I try to do a little bit, but I'm

Dan Henderson boasts a 24-0 record in mixed-martial arts competition.

The opponent takes Dan Henderson's back and places his hooks in preparation for a rear-naked choke (1). Before it's completed, Henderson rolls onto his left shoulder (2) and maneuvers out from under his foe (3). He then scrambles to his knees while underhooking the man's right arm and controlling his head (4). Next, Henderson rolls him over (5) and punches from the side-control position (6).

probably the least flexible guy. I can't touch my toes.

BB: Has that hurt your performance or caused you any injuries?

Henderson: No. I adapt to how my body is.

BB: How do you break up your training, from stand-up to the clinch to the ground? Do you separate the phases or incorporate them all in one workout?

Henderson: We separate them a little bit and bring them together. One or two days a week, we spar—mostly stand-up but we allow takedowns and fighting on the ground with the big gloves on. We don't break when we get in a clinch.

On other days, we put on MMA gloves and start on our feet, but we're not standing there sparring. We don't spend much time open; we give ourselves 10 seconds to get in a clinch. We throw light strikes and hit each other.

On other days, we'll do the same thing in MMA gloves but starting on the ground. But I like most training to be on our feet.

BB: How many times a week do you actually fight in the ring?

Henderson: We spar on the lighter days at 70 to 80 percent. At least one day a week, we spar at 100 percent.

BB: With MMA gloves?

Henderson: No. You can't spar 100 percent with MMA gloves.

BB: There's an old saying: The way you train is the way you fight. If you pull your punches in training, do you also find yourself pulling them in fights?

Henderson: I don't have that problem. I punch hard out there. In training with the big gloves, we go 100 percent, with takedowns and everything else. With grappling and wrestling, we go 100 percent. It's only the actual striking with MMA gloves that's not as hard.

BB: With 16-ounce gloves, is it difficult to get a good grip for grappling techniques?

Henderson: It's harder to take a guy down and harder to lock your hands. [During that kind of training,] I usually stay on the ground for 20 or 30 seconds, then stand back up.

BB: How many days a week do you go 100 percent?

Henderson: One day a week, sometimes two. If you go hard all the time, people will get hurt. When I say 100 percent, I'm not trying to knock the guy out, but sometimes it happens. Body shots are 100 percent; leg shots are 90 to 100 percent. But when I know it's a clean shot, I'm not going to follow through as hard.

BB: You used to be a wrestler, but it seems like you're mainly a striker now and that you use your wrestling to keep from going to the ground or to get back up if you're on the mat so you can ground and pound.

Henderson: Yeah, that's my best chance to finish the fight. I'm pretty good on submissions, as well. I guess I just haven't given myself a chance to try to submit guys in fights. It's fun for me to pound on somebody, and that's what promoters and fans like to see.

BB: What do you think of the two opposing philosophies: More is better, and less is best?

Henderson: It's always good to change things up a little bit; you don't

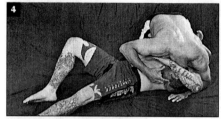

Brian Foster holds Dan Henderson in the guillotine (1). Henderson protects his neck as he pushes against the opponent's left thigh and encircles his right knee with his left arm (2). He then effects a takedown (3) and, as soon as he lands, begins to free his head from the hold (4). His escape from the guillotine extends the opponent's arm (5), enabling Henderson to transition into an arm and shoulder lock (6).

want to do the same thing because people will watch your fights and know what you're going to do. And you're not progressing as much as a fighter. But I would rather know a couple of things really well than know a whole bunch of things that I couldn't do on everybody. But you have to know [a variety of techniques] to stop submissions. Plus, it's fun learning all that stuff.

BB: Anyone who studies MMA matches can see what works: the cross-body armbar from the mount, the triangle, the heel hook, the knee bar, the *kimura*. Do you tend to focus on common denominators like those techniques?

212

Henderson: Yeah. That's pretty much my philosophy. When I teach seminars, it's the stuff I know will work.

BB: Which stand-up techniques are effective for you?

Henderson: The overhand right works well, but it has to have good timing. It's not something that you can just walk out and land on somebody. And I've been working on my body shots and left-hand jabs and hooks.

BB: What got you interested in body shots?

Henderson: Everyone was saying how well they work, and I thought I'd try them.

BB: What about right hooks to the body?

Henderson: I do them, just not as much as left hooks. I typically throw my right to the head and come back with a left to the body.

BB: Uppercuts?

Henderson: They're a big part of my boxing, more so in the clinch. I don't do a lot of uppercuts from out in the open.

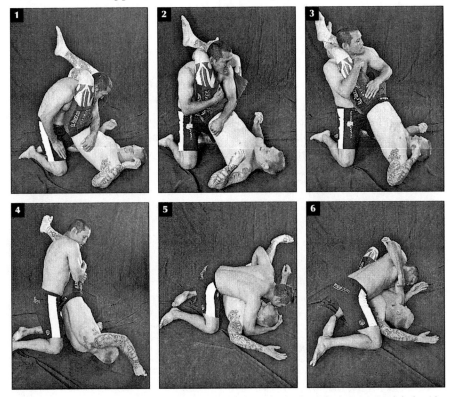

To escape from the triangle (1), Dan Henderson straightens his back while thrusting his left shoulder through the opponent's locked legs (2). He then increases the size of the opening between the man's knees (3) and slips his head under his left leg (4). Henderson releases his opponent's legs and falls on top of him (5), where he can control him or begin to ground-and-pound (6).

BB: How about elbows?

Henderson: In PRIDE, we're allowed to throw elbows, just not to the head. We can elbow the body all we want. I do a lot; most are on the ground. They're a useful tool and can get your opponent to move.

BB: Do you relegate them to secondary status?

Henderson: They're down on the list. Elbows can cut a guy and stop a fight. They don't really knock a guy out.

BB: Just about everyone in MMA does round kicks, and most fighters do front kicks. Side kicks are not used much. Are any other kicks viable in the ring?

Henderson: Sometimes I do spinning kicks in training, but I don't think I've ever done one in a fight. I got caught with one to the body just yesterday. They definitely work, but they take technique and timing.

BB: Do you think a lead-leg round kick does much damage?

Henderson: It mostly annoys the guy and gets him to react so you can set up your hands. If you're fighting a lefty, you can do a lead-leg round kick to his front leg, and it will take its toll.

BB: Do you ever use front kicks?

Henderson: Not a whole lot, but I do them in practice. The guys I train with use them, and it annoys me. I'm always moving forward, and it's easy for them to put up a leg and push me away. I don't think the front kick is a bad kick. It's useful if you're an offensive fighter and not as useful if you're defensive and trying to kick a guy from a distance.

BB: Are knees the only effective strikes you can use in a clinch?

Henderson: There are a lot of things. It depends on how your opponent is reacting. I do a lot of uppercuts from the clinch and elbows to the body to set him up. Knees are easily stopped in the clinch, but they're definitely useful.

BB: In the ring, only knees to the head seem to do damage. Knees to the body seem less effective.

Henderson: No. Knees to the body work well. It's like a boxer doing body shots—they'll wear a guy down. Knees to the thighs are more of an annoyance to get him to move, maybe to set up a takedown.

I learned a long time ago not to tell someone a technique won't work. A lot of it is the setup—how you get into position for it. That's going to be different for everybody. For example, take the overhand right. The way I get into it might not work for everybody.

If you like a move, you'll learn it and get good at it. If you don't like it, you should practice it so you don't get caught in it.

BB: With the clinch, is your strategy to get out of it and begin striking again, or to take your opponent down?

Henderson: It depends on how good he is on his feet and how tired I am. A lot of times, I'll stay in the clinch and try to beat him up.

BB: It seems that of the three stages of fighting, the clinch is least developed.

Henderson: A lot of guys get in the clinch and stop. I don't like that. I get in a clinch and fight for a while, then fight out of it. Train how you fight.

BB: Let's talk takedown defense. In your opinion, what's the key to the sprawl?

Henderson: The greatest thing is making sure you know where the guy's head is. You want to maintain control of his head—push it down while you sprawl.

BB: With respect to ground fighting, is anything other than the kimura, armbar, triangle, rear-naked choke, guillotine and heel hook effective?

Henderson: I do a lot of stuff from the half-guard and side control. From the half-guard on top, I have a good choke. It's something I discovered on my own and modified. Most of my other stuff involves getting into a position where I can beat on the guy.

BB: Do you spend much time practicing those staples of grappling?

Henderson: I don't. I do them, but I don't drill them that much. If I drill them, it's more for defense.

BB: It seems like the main styles seen in MMA are boxing, *muay Thai*, wrestling, Brazilian *jujutsu* and judo. Would you say they're the arts aspiring fighters should focus on?

Henderson: The biggest components of MMA are wrestling, kickboxing and jujutsu. Judo is a kind of wrestling, and kickboxing encompasses boxing. I think MMA is the sum of those three things, and in those three things there's so much to learn that you don't need to go outside them too much.

BB: Which art would you advise people to study first?

Henderson: Nowadays, most up-and-coming fighters are from an MMA background. I think that's the best base to have. Most trainers aren't real good at wrestling. They don't know takedowns well because they don't have a wrestling background. If everyone had to fight with a *gi*, I would say it's most beneficial to study Brazilian jujutsu, as well, but that's not the case. Wrestling without a gi is grabbing the body. Wrestling is definitely the [second] best base to have. If you were to learn one of those things growing up, I would suggest wrestling and then transitioning to the other stuff.

BB: What portion of your MMA repertoire would you teach a student

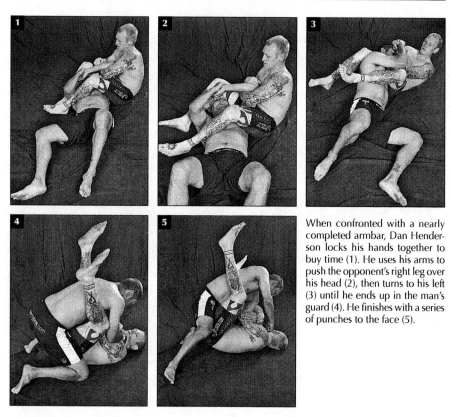

When confronted with a nearly completed armbar, Dan Henderson locks his hands together to buy time (1). He uses his arms to push the opponent's right leg over his head (2), then turns to his left (3) until he ends up in the man's guard (4). He finishes with a series of punches to the face (5).

interested in self-defense?

Henderson: I'd teach methods for controlling the guy rather than punching: getting into a clinch and taking him down, or getting behind him and controlling him. Most people aren't really good at controlling and don't know how to stop someone from controlling them.

And I'd teach ways to not get hit. And maybe to kick him in the groin.